"The 'stewardship of the mystery,' which Paul refers to as having been hidden in ages and generations past and is now revealed, is 'Christ in you the hope of glory.' Eric Johnson invites us to shed the insufficient garments of religiosity that cause us to think too small and to put on the royal robes of our largeness in Christ, which God the Father has provided in order to reveal His glory in the earth. *Christ in You* will dare and challenge you to believe that greatness awaits you when you walk by faith in the awareness of the Greater One who lives within you!"

Bishop Mark J. Chironna, M.A., Ph.D.,
Church on the Living Edge,
Orlando, Florida

"Eric's book is a refreshing reminder of the foundational elements that we need for our walk with God. It inspired me to explore my beliefs, apply truth and walk in the freedom that Jesus gave us. But more so than anything, it made me want to love God and people well."

Kelly Clark, four-time Olympian;
Olympic gold medalist and two-time Olympic
bronze medalist, snowboard halfpipe

"God never gives less than Himself to His children! *Christ in You*, by Eric Johnson, is a powerful, thought-provoking tool that teaches believers how to live *from* Jesus rather than *for* Him. If you are drawn to the majesty and mystery of authentic living, READ ON!"

Leif Hetland, president and founder,
Global Mission Awareness;
g *Through Heaven's Eyes*

CHRIST IN YOU

---+---

CHRIST IN YOU

+

WHY GOD TRUSTS YOU MORE THAN YOU TRUST YOURSELF

ERIC JOHNSON

Chosen

a division of Baker Publishing Group
Minneapolis, Minnesota

© 2015 by Eric Johnson

Published by Chosen Books
11400 Hampshire Avenue South
Bloomington, Minnesota 55438
www.chosenbooks.com

Chosen Books is a division of
Baker Publishing Group, Grand Rapids, Michigan

Printed in the United States of America

Library of Congress Cataloging-in-Publication Data is on file with the Library of Congress in Washington, D.C.

ISBN 978-0-8007-9570-2

Cover design by Amy Miller and Brianna Ailie

15 16 17 18 19 20 21   7 6 5 4 3 2 1

green press INITIATIVE

To Grandpa M. Earl Johnson, 1928–2004.
I wish everyone could meet you.
You taught us how to love people
in a way that goes beyond the desire
to protect our own reputations.

Contents

Foreword

There is a story of God unfolding in the earth right now. His story is bursting with hope and the great expectation of good things. Many believers feel hopeless about what they see in their cities and nations because they are unaware of the story of God happening around them. But I am convinced that God's heart is burning for cities and nations. He longs to reveal His glory and help those who do not yet know Him to encounter His goodness and grace.

To fulfill this mandate and accomplish His purposes in the earth, God has always awakened the Church and flowed through people. You and I are called to see the broken restored and to repair and build up wasted and desolate places.

If we as the Church are to walk in this commissioning, however, we must shift how we view certain things, because our perception will either propel us or limit us. Our mindsets dictate our choices. In other words, we must produce on the outside what we are processing on the inside. What we believe about God, therefore, and how we view His interactions in the world directly influence how we live and the impact we have.

It is imperative that we allow the Lord to reveal His heart to us and allow His Word to manifest within and through us.

God uses individuals like you and me to bring healing, life and hope. He moves through those who believe they are called to reflect His goodness and see His Kingdom established around them. He releases His Spirit through those who clearly recognize what He has assigned them to—those who walk in the revelation that Christ is in them and the hope of glory.

We are all on a journey to grasp the fullness of what this means, which is why I believe God is highlighting this topic today. I am grateful that my friend Eric Johnson has written *Christ in You*, to encourage the Church to embrace all that is available for us. Each chapter deals with a crucial truth that will propel you further in your walk with the Lord. I believe that as He transitions our mindsets from many of the issues we have viewed incorrectly in the past, the result will be an increase of heaven in and through every facet of our lives. When we surrender to the truth of the greatness He has designed us for, we will take dominion over darkness and shape society with His favor and glory.

There are promises of our Father yet to be birthed throughout the earth. I believe that truth releases these promises and that we will see the fulfillment of His Word.

Eric writes from a place of authority developed through years of faithfulness and obedience to the Lord. As senior leader of Bethel Church in Redding, California, he has poured his life out to see a community of people embrace these concepts. The fruit that has come from this passionate community of believers affects not only the world, but (perhaps even more profoundly) the city they live in. Day after day they are experiencing miracles and people encountering God, within a culture that is shifting and an atmosphere that is revolutionizing those in their region.

You and I need an internal reality founded on Kingdom revelation—an understanding of *who* we are and *whose* we are. With the tender heartbeat of our Father, the dynamic mind of Christ and the empowerment of the Holy Spirit, we will display His kindness, justice, beauty, creativity, peace, grace and wisdom. And we will see cities saved and nations transformed.

My prayer is that this book contributes to the impact of truth on our personal lives and on our mission in the earth.

Banning Liebscher, founder and director, Jesus Culture;
lead pastor, Jesus Culture Sacramento

Acknowledgments

Writing a book is not something I can do alone, by any means. I want to thank Chosen Books for taking a risk on me.

Jane Campbell, thanks for flying all the way to Redding, California, to let me know that there was a book inside me, and thanks for helping get it out of me into written form.

Trish Konieczny, thanks for your gift in editing and refining words. I am really going to miss your query boxes.

Pam Spinosi, once again you have been a massive blessing to me in helping get this book past its first stage of editing.

Last but not least, Bethel Redding church family, thanks for letting me teach and preach on the very contents of this book week after week. Your love and commitment is something I will never forget.

Introduction

The Stage Is Set

This book you are about to read is a project that began in me roughly a decade ago, and it has continued up through the present day. When it started, I was in a certain season of life in which I felt the Lord was rewiring me in a few areas. One of the areas involved my perception of Him, and how that perception affected my relationship with Him. As the rewiring process began to unfold, I felt as though I was ushered into a whole new world of understanding about what it means to be a child of the King. It was a turning point in my life spiritually and philosophically.

My rewiring did not happen overnight, but over time. Looking back, I can easily connect the dots between what the Lord was building inside me and what He is continuing to build. Sometimes the "dot" was a Scripture verse or a passage in the Bible that stood out to me, and other times the "dot" was a situation I was in or an experience I had. All these things acted as building blocks that I believe are largely compiled into what you see in the following pages.

We live in a moment when time seems to be speeding up more than ever. What is new today is out-of-date tomorrow. The effect on us is evident, both in our culture and in the way we function as a society and ultimately as believers. Traditions, customs, structures and the way we do life are being challenged in every way imaginable. The hunger for truth and authenticity is at an all-time high. The nations are on their knees, yearning for answers to problems that were inconceivable twenty years ago, let alone one hundred years ago. The stage is being set and the deck is being stacked for the ultimate prize, the time when every kingdom of this world becomes the Kingdom of our Lord. And there is only one answer to anything—Jesus Christ and the fact that He lives in you and me.

While some people decide to spend a lot of their time complaining about and criticizing people, society and the world, I have decided to spend my life pouring into people because of what I see God doing at the core of society on the planet. For me, having an awareness of history while actively living in the present and glimpsing the future is exciting. From what I see, the future looks promising. Hope is rising in the nations.

So far, even in my short life, I have seen the Church mature in ways that I have heard my forefathers and foremothers only talk about and dream about. One of the things happening across the Body of Christ is that we are moving out of certain ways of thinking and beginning to see things from a purer biblical perspective. A new breed of believers is being born, and the way they live life will look different from the way believers lived in the past. The conventional ways of thinking are being challenged, and rightfully so. The way we do ministry must change in our lifetime, and it is changing.

Isn't it interesting that it is completely normal and natural for children to think about how great they are and what they want to become? They live with such hope and confidence about what is possible in their lifetime. Sadly, once logic and reason begin to develop in them, their confidence tends to wane. Many call it reaching maturity, but it is really the slow death of what was meant to be. The people history tells us about are the ones who defied this unfortunate tendency in the human race. They made a decision to break free from the constraints of nominal thinking. They pioneered a way for whoever would choose to follow.

In our backyard we have a trampoline, as well as a mature mulberry tree that is the ultimate climbing tree. This tree was one of the major reasons we bought our house. Anytime our daughters and their friends go into the backyard, a magnetic thing takes place. They are either drawn to jumping on the trampoline or to seeing how high they can climb in the mulberry tree. No one tells them to do it, but something inside them compels them. It is normal and natural that when their eyes make contact with a tree or a trampoline, they want to find ways to climb higher or jump higher.

So it should be with those of us in the Body of Christ. In the Kingdom, there is only one direction to go, and it is from glory to glory. It should be normal for us to want to move in that direction. I believe that God's intended design called for us to be the boldest, most confident people on the planet— the kind of people who are fully aware of who they are and of whom they serve. Out of that awareness is birthed in us a divine compassion to serve the human race with the cause of Christ. Something is not right when "children" of God are walking in the opposite of that boldness, in shame and timidity. The death and resurrection of Jesus were intended to set us free from the death inherent in sin and were also the keys to our living in the abundance of the King in every area of life.

As the Body of Christ has matured and stepped into the things God has in mind, a dramatic shift has taken place. The Church has moved from an understanding of salvation to an understanding of the Kingdom. For centuries, the Church has largely focused on salvation. The main thrust has been to get people saved so they could go to heaven. What is interesting is that while the Church has spent most of its time talking about going to heaven, Jesus spent quite a bit of His time talking about bringing the Kingdom of heaven to earth.

It is good for us to talk about what God is talking about. In these pages, I want to talk about how it is the responsibility of every believer to bring the Kingdom of heaven here on earth. It is our responsibility to carry out the plan God set in motion thousands of years ago. It is our responsibility to see the name of Jesus made known in all the earth, to take things that are wrong and make them right and to bring the goodness of God into every situation. We need to spend less time elaborating on the things He did not emphasize, and instead talk about what He talked about—seeing the Kingdom come.

As you read this book, my ultimate desire for you is that you would become more aware of the depth and the width of what *Christ in you* can mean in your life and in bringing the Kingdom to earth. I have found that the more I understand *Christ in me*, the more I realize that the paradigms and mindsets I have are the very things that can limit what He intended in my life. When you and I begin to grasp *Christ in us*, we will find ourselves liberated to go higher and to move forward.

I live with a deep conviction that many in the Body of Christ need permission to climb higher and jump higher.

I believe what you will find out is that *Christ in you* is the evidence of His trust in you and your trust in Him. *Christ in you* contains all the ingredients necessary to break the status quo, challenge normalcy, eradicate apathy, abolish the fear of man and enable you to do what is humanly impossible.

1

—— + ——

In God's Image

One of my deepest desires in life is to love humanity the way Jesus did. I marvel at how He lived His life and demonstrated His love for people. Jesus started a Love Revolution. He started a movement fueled by love, and it continues to explode across the planet thousands of years later.

When we look at Jesus and His short life of 33 years, we see His life ending in the ultimate expression of love for humanity, when He gave Himself as a ransom for all. It is obvious that He had ample opportunity to become jaded or hardhearted toward people, but instead, He paid the ultimate price of laying down His life for them. One of my goals in life is that my love for people would increase over the course of my life, and not diminish. If our theology does not cause us to love humanity more and more, then we need to question our theology.

You should ask yourself these questions: *Is my heart getting harder and more calloused toward people? Or is it becoming more compassionate?* Your goal, and the goal of every believer, should be to grow in compassion and love for people as you mature in your walk with God.

Art Gallery

One of my passions in life is appreciating art and design. I highly respect things done with excellence. Sometimes I go into an art gallery and wander around to look at various pieces of art: paintings, designs, maybe a sculpture. I am always intrigued by the price at which some of these pieces are valued. Sometimes I say to myself, *No way would I pay that much for this piece of art. My daughter drew something like that in preschool.*

Suppose, however, that the artist of such a piece were to come into the art gallery and stand next to me. That would be a great opportunity for me to say, "Please tell me about this piece you've created."

The artist would then tell me what he or she was feeling and experiencing as the piece was created, and I could begin to grasp the motive behind the artwork. That would be the starting point of my being able to place a value on what was created.

I have actually had this scenario take place, where an artist told me what was in her heart as she created a certain piece, and that knowledge changed my perspective to be more like the artist's perspective. When I heard the artist describing her creative experience, something took place inside me. I began to see the piece the way the artist intended, and I acquired a value for something that I had not appreciated just a few moments before.

Whenever we do not understand a piece of art we are looking at, it is easy to criticize, judge or even dissect it in an effort to make it "understandable" to us. When we begin to get the narrative from the artist, however, our hearts and minds begin to see things we have never seen before. By the time we leave the art gallery, we feel as if our eyes have seen something we did not see when we first walked in. In many ways, until we hear the narrative of the creator, we are left to our own interpretation.

That certainly parallels the way many Christians form their perspectives. I am amazed at how many believers have developed their own narrative on something they did not create or have any part in making—humanity. We must embrace God's intent for humanity before we create our own perspective on the human race. Anytime you separate a design from the intent of its creator, you make it like yourself, or like the way you would make it, regardless of how hard you try not to. All it takes are time and life experiences to craft the design to your own liking.

In His Image

Though we encounter abstract thoughts and ideas in art and in life that are hard for us to grasp, it is important to go back to their conception, to their roots, to gain an accurate picture of the idea itself. Let's do that with humanity. Let's go back to the beginning and see what God had in His heart toward humanity from its conception.

> Then God said, "Let Us make man in Our image, according to Our likeness; let them have dominion over the fish of the sea, over the birds of the air, and over the cattle, over all the earth and over every creeping thing that creeps on the earth." So God created man in His own image; in the image of God He created him; male and female He created them. Then

God blessed them, and God said to them, "Be fruitful and multiply; fill the earth and subdue it; have dominion over the fish of the sea, over the birds of the air, and over every living thing that moves on the earth."

And God said, "See, I have given you every herb that yields seed which is on the face of all the earth, and every tree whose fruit yields seed; to you it shall be for food. Also, to every beast of the earth, to every bird of the air, and to everything that creeps on the earth, in which there is life, I have given every green herb for food"; and it was so. Then God saw everything that He had made, and indeed it was very good. So the evening and the morning were the sixth day.

Genesis 1:26–31

Let's take a moment to look at verse 26: "Then God said, 'Let Us make man in Our *image*, according to Our *likeness*'" (emphasis added). God creates the heavens and the earth in the first five days of Creation. On the sixth day, He does something unique that we need to grasp. He decides to make man in His *image*. The word *image* carries the definition of a "shadow, a phantom, figuratively an illusion, resemblance, and representative."[1] To be created in the image of God is to resemble Him and to be His representative. The word *likeness* means "resemblance, model, shape, fashion and manner."[2] Since being created in the image of God means that we resemble Him and are His representatives, we are to carry ourselves in such a way that we act like Him. This was God's intent for humanity from the beginning. It is vital that we do not forget what God had in mind for us from the start.

1. "Lexicon: Strong's H6754," Blue Letter Bible online, ©2014 Sowing Circle, https://www.blueletterbible.org/lang/lexicon/lexicon.cfm?Strongs=H6754&t=KJV.
2. "Lexicon: Strong's H1823," Blue Letter Bible online, ©2014 Sowing Circle, https://www.blueletterbible.org/lang/lexicon/lexicon.cfm?Strongs=H1823&t=KJV.

Take Dominion

Humanity was created in God's image. God had the idea in mind that we would take dominion over the earth. In Revelation 12:7–9 we read,

> And war broke out in heaven: Michael and his angels fought with the dragon; and the dragon and his angels fought, but they did not prevail, nor was a place found for them in heaven any longer. So the great dragon was cast out, that serpent of old, called the Devil and Satan, who deceives the whole world; he was cast to the earth, and his angels were cast out with him.

When God told Adam and Eve to take dominion over the earth, it was because they did not yet have dominion. I think it is incredibly fascinating that one of the reasons God created humanity in His very image and likeness, to represent Him on this planet, was for the express purpose of taking dominion. One of the indisputable aspects of God's heart from the beginning was that people would partner with Him by carrying out their God-given mission and mandate to take dominion over the earth. This alone allows us to see that God wanted us to co-labor with Him in this cause. I believe that this pronouncement from Genesis 1:28 is where we must stop and listen to the Artist articulate what His "painting" is all about. This is the moment of Creation that proves that people have the ability and capacity to do good on the earth.

In this moment, God's command came forth from an idea He had that humanity would accomplish the task of taking dominion over the earth. It was in the beginning, when humanity just got started, that God commissioned us to carry out this task. What happened after that moment is written in the history books for all to read. Although the journey of humanity has since included the Fall of man, wars and famines, kingdoms rising and falling, and all kinds of twists and turns, the whole thing started with the notion that people have the capacity to accomplish the intent of God's heart. We need to live every day from this understanding.

The Fall of Man

Since you and I are standing in this place in history thousands of years after the creation of humanity, we can look back and see things from a historical and biblical perspective. We can see that one of the major moments that altered history was the Fall of man, when Adam and Eve sinned against God (see Genesis 3:1–7). That moment set the course of human history in a direction that God had not intended. Sin entered into the equation, which set the stage for restoration and reconciliation through the death and resurrection of Jesus Christ.

It is common to assume that the Fall changed God's original plan. But if we think that the entrance of sin into the world was more powerful than God's plan or His sovereignty, then our view of God is inferior to what Scripture details for us. The Fall took humanity on a crash course, teaching us how sin and death can wreak havoc in our lives when we tolerate sin. The only way to rise above sin and death and step into a place of righteousness is through confessing our sins and putting our faith in Jesus Christ. His death and resurrection restore us to a place of covenant with God. As Jesus said in John 14:6, "I am the way, the truth, and the life. No one comes to the Father except through Me."

The only way to righteousness is through Jesus because He is the way and the truth that brings life. There is no second option; the only option is simple and concrete—it is Jesus.

Romans 1:16–17 tells us that the Gospel of Christ "is the power of God to salvation for everyone who believes, for the Jew first and also for the Greek. For in it the righteousness of God is revealed from faith to faith; as it is written, 'The just shall live by faith.'" When I confess my sin and put my faith in God, a veil is removed from my eyes and I can see His glory. Living by faith opens our eyes so that we can both see His righteousness and understand His heart toward us.

The Capacity to Do Good

Romans 3:10 says, "There is none righteous, no, not one.'" Whether saved or not, human beings are not "good." To say that they are, and that human sin is not a problem, is to undercut the need for the terrible and unspeakable sacrifice of Jesus Christ on the cross.

But it is important to differentiate between being righteous and doing good. These are two different things. The only way to righteousness, as we just discussed, is through confession of sin and faith in the death and resurrection of Jesus Christ. There is no other way to the Father. That much is simple and clear.

When it comes to doing good, however, every human being, saved or unsaved, has the ability to do good things on the earth. It is not hard to look around and see clear demonstrations of this. People who are not followers of Jesus Christ are accomplishing great things such as loving the unlovely, feeding the hungry, clothing the naked and helping bring solutions to the issues humanity faces. You can find professed atheists who are doing good on the earth. The reason for this is that every human being is created in the image of God, even those who have not yet experienced the second birth in Christ. Sometimes it even seems—as dismaying as this is—that people who are not followers of Jesus can be doing more good on the earth than believers are doing.

In Matthew 7:11, Jesus said, "If you then, being evil, know how to give good gifts to your children, how much more will your Father who is in heaven give good things to those who ask Him!" Then in Matthew 12:35, He said, "A good man out of the good treasure of his heart brings forth good things." Jesus lays it out, saying that even those who are "evil" still know how to give good gifts. He also says a "good" man brings forth good things. Either way, the capacity to do good things is in everyone.

I think there is an intrinsic desire inside every person to do something good, and that desire originates from the truth that we are all created in the image of God, whether we realize it or not. Though sin came into the world, sin does not get rid of the image of God in us. It tarnishes, dilutes and erodes it, but it does not do away with it. If an individual tolerates and engages in sin, it will continue to bring death, as noted in Romans 6:23: "For the wages of sin is death, but the gift of God is eternal life in Christ Jesus our Lord." But it will not erase the image of God in that person.

Some feel that if we keep looking for the image of God in people and do not emphasize sin enough, we start to diminish or ignore the death inherent in sin. The opposite is true. When we begin to see clearly the original intent God had in mind when He created mankind in His image, we truly begin to see in contrast to that the absolute ugliness of sin and death. The more I become aware of the image of God in people, the more disgusted I become with sin.

To illustrate this, let's say my entire experience of the norm is a cup of dirty water. I have no concept of, or previous experience with, a cup of clean water. I have no way to compare dirty water to clean water because my paradigm consists of only one cup of dirty water. That is all I have ever known. When I am exposed to a cup of clean water, however, I become aware of something that I previously did not know existed. I become aware that there is such a thing as clean water. When I learn what a cup of clean water is, I can then understand that what I previously thought was the norm—dirty water—is actually an inferior version.

Likewise, when I am exposed to the goodness of God toward us, I become aware of something that I previously did not know existed. I become aware that in His goodness, He created us—all of us—in His image. If in my previous experience, I focused largely on the unredeemed aspects of humanity, and then I begin to see God's image in people (both the redeemed and the unredeemed), it puts everything in a different perspective. Once I begin to understand God's original intent for humanity and that we are created in His image, it highlights even more clearly the absolute death that sin brings.

Let me say again that just because a person can do good things does not mean that person is securing his or her eternity in Christ. Being created in the image of God and possessing the ability to do good things on the earth does not make anyone righteous or win him or her brownie points with God. Knowing this should heighten the realization in us of our need for a Savior. The entrance of sin into the world broke the relationship humanity had with God, and the death and resurrection of His Son, Jesus, restored that relationship.

You and I have a responsibility as believers to see humanity in the light of God's original design. That is why I have chosen to spend time sowing into people's lives rather than constantly being critical of them and finding fault. The more I realize that people are designed to accomplish good things on the earth, the more I can see God's image in them. Yes, each of us needs a Savior, and having the image of God in us is a different thing from standing righteous before Him. But Jesus made a way for us to be forgiven and to live in a place where we can fully experience and carry out what God intended in His original design.

Shaping Our Society

As part of the Body of Christ, we should not view humanity solely through the lens of seeing people as sinners. There should also be a lens we look through that helps us see that people are created in the image of God.

Leaders in the Church, government and in all parts of society should keep in mind that people are designed for and can do good. Daily, we are confronted with the effects of sin and death on society. The way we live our lives helps shape our culture, and many of us participate in government. As believers, we need to exert all our influence to set things up that lead people to a place of knowing God and of being aware that they are designed for good. We need to work toward having all laws and guidelines arise from the core value of helping people realize they were created in God's image. Systems should be put in place to help restore that image in them. Wherever we have influence in society, our strong emphasis should be on helping to expose them to what God had in mind when He created them.

Imagine a legal system designed around the core value that people are created in the image of God. That is not to say that sin in such a system would be dealt with passively. We ought not tolerate sin. But what if, when people were convicted of a crime, they were not just put into a cell block to serve out their time? What if inmates were put into a system designed to make them aware of who God created them to be? What if our prison system helped restore dignity and honor back to its inmates? What if this initiated true repentance on all levels: to God and to the ones they have hurt or committed the crime against?

What if our educational systems were geared toward letting students know that they are designed to do good on the earth? What if more time were spent exposing students to difficult situations and assigning them the task of helping bring solutions? What if schools diligently searched out the uniqueness and gifts in each student and let the results be the guiding compass for that child's years of education? What if teachers partnered together so that when a child moved from one grade to the next, the new teacher would be made aware of the child's uniqueness and gifts so the teacher could continue to pour into the child with that in mind? What if there were a value system created not just based on academic grades, but on how a student stewarded the giftings, callings and identity he or she possessed?

If we are going to navigate the sin and evil rampant on the earth and help usher the Kingdom into every level of society, we have to recognize how important it is to see the image of God in every person we meet. If we do not realize the importance of that image in them, we most likely will deal with sin and evil from the basis of a short-term mindset that has as its goal alleviating the consequences of sin but not helping the person become healthy and whole as well as saved.

I believe that if we as believers have a good grasp of seeing the image of God in people, then we will cultivate a deep love for them that does not have an agenda attached. People will not become the objects of our agenda. Rather, we will see the uniqueness of each person, and we will spend our lives simply loving people into the Kingdom. That all by itself is bound to have an eternal effect on our churches, government and society.

Seeing Humanity through God's Eyes

When I look at the life of Christ, the message He preached and the people He preached it to have always caught my attention. He dealt with sin head-on, and numerous times in the gospels He preached the message, "Repent, for the Kingdom of heaven is at hand." It seems that the very people He was telling to repent were the same ones who wanted to be around Him. His message drew people in, instead of pushing them away.

In fact, Jesus was accused of being among the kind of people who needed to repent. People were calling Him "one of them" in Matthew 11:19: "The Son of Man came eating and drinking, and they say, 'Look, a glutton and a winebibber, a friend of tax collectors and sinners!'"

Usually when you are accused of being "one of them," it is because you have spent a good length of time with the people in that group. Jesus unapologetically spent quite a bit of time with sinners. He became famous for this. To the religious leaders of His time, he was guilty by association. To the people, He was a friend and Savior.

Our job is to live our lives as Jesus did, so that people who are lost and hurting know they have a friend in us. If we are not living that way, our perspective on humanity needs to shift. A true Kingdom perspective on humanity is not driven only by the sin you see in people; it is driven by seeing in them who God created them to be. And once we have His light in us, we are not guilty by association when we are with them.

Let's learn to love the "hell" out of people, even if those who do not understand pronounce us guilty by association.

There is a good chance that if you truly love humanity the way God loves humanity, you will be accused of guilt by association at best, and heresy at worst. If your theology does not cause you to love people more, however, then you must question your theology. It is tragic that as many believers mature in their walk with the Lord, they become more distant from people in general and draw lines that create an us-versus-them paradigm. When believers allow salvation to make them feel superior to the rest of humanity, they start creating little worlds to keep themselves at a safe distance from the "them" who make up everyone else outside their narrow Christian circles. Yet we were not called to create our own cities, but to go into the cities of this world as servants of the King and bring His light into the darkness.

It is extremely challenging to bring His light into the cities of this world when you carry an us-versus-them approach. Becoming a believer in Jesus does not make you superior to anybody else; it qualifies you for heaven and enables you to carry out the Great Commission, bringing the life of heaven into every situation. As we look at the life of Jesus, we see that He was constantly demonstrating this by serving humanity. Look at Acts 10:38 (emphasis added): "God anointed Jesus of Nazareth with the Holy Spirit and with power, who went about *doing good* and *healing all* who were oppressed by the devil, for God was with Him."

Notice that Jesus went about doing good and bringing healing into people's lives. Now is the time for those of us in the Body of Christ to get off our personal soapboxes and spend more time doing likewise. So much liberty comes when we realize that by carrying an attitude of doing good on the earth, we can live our lives in such a way that we are advancing the

Kingdom of God and making the name of Christ known in all the earth. When Jesus went about doing good and healing all, He was on a mission to reveal the heart of God toward humanity. So are we, if we are living as He did.

God's Goodness Leads to Repentance

What would happen if we set aside our typical Christian agenda of trying to get people to pray a prayer of salvation and adopted an approach in which we purely loved people? What would happen if we fully embraced the concept of Romans 2:4, that "the goodness of God leads you to repentance"?

My wife and I were youth pastors for around nine years. For six of those years, we were in Weaverville, California. When we first took over the position there, around 75 young people attended our youth group. That made up 15 to 20 percent of the only high school in Weaverville. We stepped into a youth ministry that was already carrying a lot of momentum and life. Over the course of the next three or four years, though, the youth group shrank drastically. Many of our youth graduated from high school during that time and moved on, and somehow we were not yet reaching the next generation. There were times when we found ourselves with just a handful of young people on a Wednesday night. I remember one night when only three to four youth showed up. We decided to take them down to the local ice-cream shop and buy them all a treat, which made them happy. But I was not feeling it. It was so challenging to feel encouraged.

For me personally, it was a tough season. On the morning following that meeting when only a few attended, I thought seriously of resigning—and not for the first time. I probably resigned a thousand times in that season. I was feeling like a failure as a leader, and everything in me wanted to end the madness.

As we were going through that, I remember coming across the truth in Romans 2:4, that the goodness of God leads people to repentance. My wife and I called a leadership meeting with our adult leaders. The entire meeting, we talked about how we were going to stop all our little programs and clear out the calendar. We were going to start focusing on building relationship with young people, and we were going to spend most of our time letting the goodness of God lead them to repentance.

At one point in that meeting, I remember telling our leaders something along the lines of, "I don't want any of us to tell the young people to quit smoking, quit sleeping around or stop going to parties. Instead, let's grab their hands and get them as close to God as possible."

We all made an agreement that the only thing on our agenda would be to build relationships and help area youth see the goodness of God. It was fun to see what took place in the months and years following that meeting. I watched with interest as we all got used to saying less to the youth and doing more with them. In some ways, we had to rewire ourselves to see them differently.

I remember finding myself loving the kids more, largely because I was not so focused on their sin. I was more focused on who they were. That enabled me to stand right by them and be their friend, even as they were in the midst of trying to figure things out. At times it got really messy. Some of the kids made poor decisions that caused all of us, not to mention them, a lot of pain. But we decided that we would steward our relationship with them over anything else. And because they were experiencing the goodness and love of God through us, we began to see some cool stuff happen. Young people were repenting, getting right with God and becoming believers because they were experiencing God's goodness.

One young man was notorious for his lawlessness. He did not seem to have any moral conscience at all. Since I was deciding to let the goodness of God do the work, I got really good at not flinching when he told me what he had done the previous weekend, activities that usually consisted of drugs, sex or being involved in some dangerous situation. Over time, his language changed from flaunting his crazy lifestyle to "I can't live this way anymore." What was happening? The goodness of God was beginning to rebuild a moral conscience in him. Conviction was getting louder and louder as he was experiencing love from us and from God.

Over the next couple years, we saw a whole new generation of young people become a community of believers. My wife and I, along with our team, saw God build the ministry, and we got to do our part and watch it happen. By the time we handed off the youth ministry to the next youth pastors, we had between seventy and eighty youth who called the youth group their home. It was never about the numbers, but the numbers were a testament to what God had done in the lives of many young people. I firmly believe that when a person is confronted with the goodness of God, the natural response is to repent and ultimately change the direction of his or her life.

We should never underestimate the goodness of God. If your faith in the goodness of God is not growing over time, then it might be good to find out what your faith is about. One of the core values we carry is to stay fully aware of the goodness of God, because we all live in a world that seems to feast on what is wrong with everything. There exists a huge appetite for bad news. One way to combat an appetite for bad news is to starve it and create instead an appetite for what is good and right. That never means we become ignorant of the problems that face us. It simply means we decide to carry a faith in our hearts for what is possible so that it defies the problems instead of ignoring them.

Conduits for Heaven

As we conclude this first chapter, take some time to ask yourself these questions:

1. Do you love people because the Bible instructs you to love others?
2. Do you love people because you genuinely love humanity and can see the image of God in others?

If you find yourself in a place where rather than feeling genuine love for people, you feel more of an obligation to love humanity, then this is a great time to seek the Lord and ask Him to give you the same compassion for humanity that Jesus possessed. This is a perfect moment to begin to renew your mind about humanity. True love is not obligatory; rather, it comes from a deep place in your heart.

Be diligent to find out what it is that hinders you from genuinely loving people. If your search reveals a place of pain inside you that was caused by an experience or circumstance in your past, then this is a perfect time to invite God into that area of your life to heal and restore you.

Make sure that you are living in freedom so that your love for humanity is turned on, not turned off. This will enable you to live in such a way that you will find yourself acting as a conduit for heaven. You will find yourself seeing the image of God in others and letting God's goodness, expressed through you, draw them to repentance. Let's pursue the freedom to carry the kind of love for humanity that loves the "hell" out of people.

2

+

The Greatest Mystery Revealed

Now that we have established that all humanity was created in the image of God, with the capacity to do good, let's go a step further and look at the condition of redeemed humanity. God is a master builder. He builds line upon line and precept upon precept. In the forward movement that results, a shifting occurs in the minds of believers as a result of what the Holy Spirit is doing. The Holy Spirit presents us with new paradigms, but it is up to us to embrace them. As these new paradigms are being released and as we embrace them, we begin to see things we did not see before. As if blinders had been removed from our eyes, we see the same things we saw before, but in an entirely different way.

In my life as a believer, I have noticed something taking place globally in the Body of Christ. Believers have begun to put great emphasis on the revelation of the Kingdom of heaven. The Kingdom of heaven has always been part of our language, ever since Jesus preached that "the kingdom of heaven is at hand!" (Matthew 3:2). But something is different now; we are beginning to see this concept in a new way. Our eyes are beginning to open more to what the Kingdom can look like "at hand" in society.

Since Reformation times, the Body of Christ has put a lot of emphasis on the gospel of salvation, which largely focuses on getting people "saved" so that they will spend their eternity in heaven. Now, however, the Body of Christ is becoming more aware of the gospel of the Kingdom. Jesus made emphasizing this a major priority in His time on earth. Throughout the gospels, He is found leading the charge to help people see the Kingdom of God come here on this earth.

Seeing the Kingdom come means that whatever it looks like in heaven is what it needs to look like here on earth. Jesus entrusts the knowledge of His ways and His thoughts to His people so that we will apply them in every area of our lives to usher in the Kingdom, whether it be in the area of health, government, education, the workplace or our home life. Our mandate is to see that in every area, the ways of His Kingdom are ushered in on the earth.

The gospel of salvation is *in* the gospel of the Kingdom, but the gospel of the Kingdom encompasses more than just salvation. This does not diminish or devalue salvation; rather, it highlights it and reveals the depth and the breadth of what salvation is and what it leads to.

When a paradigm shift like this takes place in our minds, another layer of truth and revelation opens up to us as believers. Colossians 1:27 (NIV) reads, "To them God has chosen to make known among the Gentiles the glorious riches of this mystery, which is Christ in you, the hope of glory." This is one of the most revolutionary verses in the Bible. As you can probably tell from this book's title, the key phrase I want to consider is *Christ in you*. It communicates something every believer must understand.

Over the centuries, humanity has shown an intense longing to worship a god. This desire has led people to the highest points of the earth in an attempt to worship some lofty being, or to the depths of the earth in the hope of finding the answer buried there. People have erected all manner of temples, mosques and monuments in the hope of creating a place where they could meet with a god.

In this process, history has recorded people doing all manner of bizarre things with their bodies and minds in an attempt to position themselves to please their gods. For some, pleasing their god (their idol) does not involve worshiping in a particular place, so much as it involves worshiping an earthly possession or position. That could involve money, people, power or fame, but whatever it is, it shows that inside every person there exists a desire to commit wholeheartedly to *something*, seen or unseen.

Everyone desires a god, and the only true fulfillment of this desire is Jesus, the only true God. The Bible states that His is the name above all names, King of kings and Lord of lords. After we sift through all the other "god options," we will find that only He is the way, the truth and the life. Only He will satisfy this longing inside us to worship. And once we realize that truth, wherever we go, He is with us and *within* us.

Until the point in time when Paul wrote his letter to the Colossians, for most of humanity the idea of God living inside them was never even a concept that entered their minds. Society in general had been set up to expect that a god would dwell in a tent or in a temple. So when Paul wrote that the greatest mystery had been revealed, that Christ was now *in* them, that concept started a whole new way of life for believers. A new understanding dawned in them as they began to realize that because of the cross and resurrection, each of them had become the very temple God lived in. The same realization needs to dawn in us today.

Introducing Wisdom

When most believers read Colossians 1:27 about Christ being in us, the hope of glory, they generally interpret it to mean, "Now that Christ is in me, it means I get to go to heaven when my time on earth has come to an end." Although this is very true, I would like to suggest that there is more to this truth that Christ lives in you and me. When we read "Christ in you," it is good to understand that it means more than that we get to go to heaven. Since Christ is in us, let's see what that means from now until the day comes when our time on earth is done.

Some of the keys to understanding what it means are found in the Old Testament. Wisdom, present throughout the Old Testament right from the start—in fact, at Creation itself—is a vital key to understanding what Christ in us can mean. The Spirit of God working within us is another important key that enables us to walk out in wisdom all that Christ in us means. Craftsmanship, expressed through developing and using our skills and abilities, is also key to bringing the Kingdom of heaven to earth through Christ in us. Craftsmanship even has the power to tear down strongholds and bring freedom.

Let's look at these keys a little more closely, starting with wisdom. Read Proverbs 8:22–31:

> The LORD possessed me at the beginning of His way,
> Before His works of old.
> I have been established from everlasting,
> From the beginning, before there was ever an earth.

When there were no depths I was brought forth,
When there were no fountains abounding with water.
Before the mountains were settled,
Before the hills, I was brought forth;
While as yet He had not made the earth or the fields,
Or the primal dust of the world.
When He prepared the heavens, I was there,
When He drew a circle on the face of the deep,
When He established the clouds above,
When He strengthened the fountains of the deep,
When He assigned to the sea its limit,
So that the waters would not transgress His command,
When He marked out the foundations of the earth,
Then I was beside Him as a master craftsman;
And I was daily His delight,
Rejoicing always before Him,
Rejoicing in His inhabited world,
And my [wisdom's] delight was with the sons of men.

This passage is a great description of the creation process. It shows the role that wisdom played in the creation of the universe. When God created the heavens and the earth, wisdom was right there to make sure everything was done perfectly, and it was. The entire sequence of Creation had to be done in order or the whole thing would have fallen apart. Obviously, water had to be created before fish were created. Vegetation had to be created before the animals. As you dive into the details of Creation, you will find that wisdom did a masterful job of making it all work. One thing to note when it comes to wisdom is that it is an integral part of Creation itself. Wisdom was not standing there watching; it was extremely engaged in the process of creation. It is just astounding!

In this passage from Proverbs 8, wisdom is portrayed as a "master craftsman" (verse 30). I am not sure we understand the depth of meaning in that title, but I recently had an experience that brought it home to me. I went to New Zealand to do a conference in the Northland, a captivating region in so many ways. Its natural beauty is off the charts. The people are fun, and they love life. I felt right at home. During the conference, I was presented with a very nice, rare gift from a Maori master craftsman. The gift was a *patu*, a tribal weapon that is a uniquely designed club with multiple uses in battle. It can also be used as a way to project the voice when held in a certain way near the chin. As I was receiving this gift from the master craftsman, I realized it was no ordinary gift. Its maker was a genuinely humble man who carried a special anointing. I was blown away by my encounter with him. I later learned that he took an entire month off work to make the *patu* for me. Some of the New Zealanders were telling me they had never even seen a *patu* made by a Maori master craftsman because it is such a rarity. The design and attention to detail are remarkable; the carvings are laid out to create a stunning overall look. As I held the *patu* in my hands, it was obvious to me that it was not just "made." This *patu* was *crafted*.

In the last verse of the passage, verse 31, we read that the delight of God was with the "sons of men." People were the design God crafted that gave Him the most delight. This is the foundation of thought you and I must live from as believers. He delights in *you*! He is crazy about *you*, and that is how it was from the beginning of all time. Often we fail to realize this truth that our Father is the proudest Dad in the universe, and He has your picture in all your amazingness on His refrigerator. God loves to show off His kids. In Genesis, after He created man, He said, "It is good." He said it because creation, especially His creation of mankind, really is good.

The Spirit of Wisdom

In the book of Exodus, as the nation of Israel is wandering the wilderness, Moses gets the download from God on building a place for Him to dwell. The revelation of God living inside you had not yet been revealed. That concept was still a mystery, and would remain a mystery for a long time. As Israel journeyed in the wilderness, though, it was in God's heart to live among His people. When Moses realized that he would need some help to build this place for God to dwell in, God gave him instructions in Exodus 31:1–3 (emphasis added):

> Then the LORD spoke to Moses, saying: "See, I have called by name Bezalel the son of Uri, the son of Hur, of the tribe of Judah. And I have filled him with the *Spirit of God,* in *wisdom,* in *understanding,* in *knowledge,* and in all manner of workmanship.

This is considered by some as the first time that the Bible mentions someone being filled with the Spirit of God, and this person was a craftsman. Not the leader of a nation, not a religious leader, not even Moses! It was a man who was good with his hands in different manners of workmanship. This gives us incredible insight into how God plans to advance the Kingdom. In this story in Exodus, He is going to use this craftsman, who would be tasked with building the elaborate tent that would eventually become the dwelling place of God.

We looked earlier at how inside every human heart there exists the desire to worship a god. I also believe that inside the heart of every believer there exists this desire to serve the Lord and help advance the Kingdom. This story in Exodus gives us a beautiful example of God using the most unassuming person as the key individual who would build His dwelling place. This is incredible in so many ways. It gives us a glimpse of the kind of people whom God likes to use to advance the Kingdom.

This one moment in history should eradicate any thought you may have had that God is not going to use you. Often we have our own ideas of whom God wants to use. Usually, we think He will use the famous people or the leader of a church somewhere. But we cannot limit advancing the Kingdom to whomever we think God will use. We must understand that God's intention is for all of humanity to advance the Kingdom. Everyone can have a part in the great privilege of seeing the Kingdom of heaven come to earth.

We all tend to have our own limited idea of "ministry" and what it will look like. I believe that one of the reasons we have not seen the Kingdom manifest in different parts of society is that we have a limited understanding of what ministry is and how God plans to touch society. In other words, our limited idea is too small. Ministry is not about what you do, as much as it is about who you are. And once you find out who you are, everything you do in life has the potential and capacity to be ministry.

If our understanding of advancing the Kingdom is also limited to the idea of getting everyone saved and healed, then we will fall short of seeing the fullness of what God had in mind. Ministry goes far beyond counting up salvations.

A number of years ago, God asked our leadership team here at Bethel a question: "What does it look like after everyone gets saved and healed?"

We did not have an answer because we began to realize that our perspective of the Kingdom was largely focused on getting people saved and healed, and we had not really thought about what it looked like after that. As a team, we began to change our conversations and to pray into this great question God had asked us.

We are still on that journey as a team, but we feel we have begun to see what it could look like for the Kingdom to touch a city on all levels. One of the things we learned about our role as a church body is that one aspect of that role involves serving our city's fathers and mothers. As my dad put it, "We serve with the heart of a king."

Our goal is not to rule and reign over our city. Rather, we aim to serve our city and help in all areas, ranging from taking care of the poor all the way to contributing to solutions that help solve the financial and social issues facing our city. How do we position ourselves to contribute to solutions? That involves just what we have been talking about—the wisdom of the Holy Spirit, combined with craftsmanship.

Let's return for a moment to the examples in Exodus. In chapters 31–39, you can read about the incredible process that took place in building God's dwelling place and everything in it. God knew exactly what He wanted when it came to building a tent for Himself. The craftsman Bezalel was filled with the Spirit of God, but God also gave wisdom to some other people in the process. Take a look at another moment in the building process:

> All the women who were gifted artisans spun yarn with their hands, and brought what they had spun, of blue, purple, and scarlet, and fine linen. And all the women whose hearts stirred with wisdom spun yarn of goats' hair.
>
> Exodus 35:25–26

Notice that the women's hearts were stirred with *wisdom*. From that place of wisdom, they were able to take goats' hair and make yarn out of it. Wisdom enabled them to take something as common as goats' hair and make it into something of value and purpose.

I would like to suggest that wisdom is much more than just good advice and instruction. It has the capacity to take something as mundane as goats' hair and utilize it in such a way that it advances the Kingdom. God emphasized that these women's hearts were being stirred with wisdom. Through that, He shows us that when we carry His Spirit and wisdom, it touches our everyday lives and positions us to help advance His Kingdom. This makes me wonder how many times we walk right past the mundane things in life and fail to realize that when wisdom is involved, those are the very things that can help establish God's Kingdom on earth. In this case it was goats' hair. Wow. Not something you would think of as Kingdom advancing, is it?

I want to challenge you to look around and really see the common things in life, and then think about what you can do with those things when you have Christ living in you. Maybe you are in the business world and you need a breakthrough. The solution may be as simple and as common as goats' hair; you just need the God-given wisdom to see it. Perhaps you are a teacher with some really challenging kids in your classroom, and you are looking for ways to succeed with them. The solution may be simpler than you expect, and may involve something you already have on hand. Again, you just need the wisdom to see it.

Whatever challenge you face, the solution is in you and around you because wisdom through the Holy Spirit is in you. Christ is in you.

Equipped with Excellence

Now let's look at Exodus 39:43: "Then Moses looked over all the work, and indeed they had done it; as the LORD had commanded, just so they had done it. And Moses blessed them." Here we see Moses taking a tour of all the work Bezalel and his company of people had done. After Moses saw everything, he noted that it had been done exactly as the Lord wanted it.

I can only imagine the excitement Moses felt in that moment, as he saw firsthand in the natural what God had shown him in the spiritual. Everything had been done with excellence and precision because a craftsman named Bezalel had been equipped with the Spirit of God in wisdom. Wisdom is a vehicle from which excellence comes.

As the attention of the Church becomes more focused on seeing the Kingdom of God come and seeing His will be done on earth, I have a growing conviction that the example of Bezalel will become really important for the Body of Christ. He is the earliest biblical reference to the Spirit of God residing in someone in wisdom. The manifestation of the Spirit in him showed up in the excellence of what he did with his hands and in his ability and skill to work with different materials.

It is hard not to think about the possible ramifications of this in our day, in this age of technology, architecture, corporate structures, inventions and innovations. There are ideas, sounds and designs in heaven that have yet to manifest on this earth. Imagine what can happen along those lines when believers realize who lives inside them!

When we realize the full extent of our partnership with heaven, what will come out of individual believers and the Body of Christ as a whole? It will be as in the days of Moses and Bezalel. Moses saw what God had in mind, and Bezalel was able to carry it out and build it. We, too, will carry out with wisdom the things that the Spirit shows us are in the mind of God. And like Bezalel, we will be equipped with excellence for the task.

The Craftsmen Are Coming

We have seen the role of wisdom in Creation and how wisdom played a vital part in the unfolding of that story. We have seen the role of wisdom in the life of a master craftsman named Bezalel, who was filled with the Spirit and was able to create something that was important to God and His relational covenant with Israel. The word *craftsman* actually is used in numerous places in the Bible. It is generally understood to mean someone who was good at whatever it was he did. In some cases it is used to describe people like Bezalel who were good with their hands, especially when it came to working with wood, metal and stone. But let's look at another interesting use of the word in Zechariah 1:18–21:

> Then I raised my eyes and looked, and there were four horns. And I said to the angel who talked with me, "What are these?"
>
> So he answered me, "These are the horns that have scattered Judah, Israel, and Jerusalem."
>
> Then the LORD showed me four craftsmen. And I said, "What are these coming to do?"
>
> So he said, "These are the horns that scattered Judah, so that no one could lift up his head; but the craftsmen are coming to terrify them, to cast out the horns of the nations that lifted up their horn against the land of Judah to scatter it."

Zechariah is having a series of visions, and this one in particular shows the role of craftsmen. He sees four horns that are demonic strongholds of the enemy. These strongholds have scattered three locations, and the result of this oppression was that these places could not lift up their heads. Whenever you see someone with his head held low, it usually is a sign that he is not doing well, is feeling discouraged and is not looking forward to anything. That was the reality for these three places. They were filled not with hope and life, but with oppression by these strongholds.

As Zechariah surveys the situation, he looks over and sees four craftsmen who are coming to terrorize the demonic strongholds. What an interesting thing in that God chooses to use craftsmen, out of all types of people, to destroy the enemy. We saw in Exodus the role the craftsmen played in helping advance the Kingdom by building the tent for God to dwell in. Now we see "craftsmen" terrorizing the enemy and bringing freedom to these three locations.

Let's keep reading in Zechariah 2:1–2:

> Then I raised my eyes and looked, and behold, a man with a measuring line in his hand. So I said, "Where are you going?"
> And he said to me, "To measure Jerusalem, to see what is its width and what is its length."

Immediately following the craftsmen destroying the strongholds of the enemy, an angel of the Lord comes and makes measurements for the rebuilding of the city. I would like to suggest that walking in wisdom ushers in liberation, and that heaven responds by partnering and accomplishing the will of God on the earth. The angel of the Lord did not come before or during the destruction of the demonic stronghold; it happened afterward. In a way, heaven was responding to the craftsmen doing their job. We tend to wait for the assistance of heaven before we do something. This vision reveals a different approach. It was not until the craftsmen had terrorized the strongholds that heaven responded to the situation.

We see a New Testament expression of this in Ephesians 3:10, which reads, "to the intent that now the manifold wisdom of God might be made known by the church to the principalities and powers in the heavenly places." The word *manifold* carries the meaning of multifaceted or multidimensional, like the famous multicolored coat of Joseph. The word *wisdom* here means "the intelligence of God." This verse says that the multidimensional intelligence of God will be made known by the believers to all powers in the heavenly places. One of the responsibilities of every believer is to demonstrate the intelligence of God. This is a profound revelation of what God has in mind for each believer. We are to carry and live out the intelligence of God, which will terrorize the demonic strongholds.

I believe the desire to rebuild cities and society is in the heart of every person whose head is lifted up and not held low. Any human being who is full of life and hope normally wants to contribute to society and make it a better place. You will notice that in the Church, the strategy for winning the nations has been changing. Instead of going into the nations and bringing in "our" way of doing things, we are going in and setting people free, which results in their lifting up their heads. When you have a person in any nation who lifts up his or her head, you then have a person who naturally wants to begin rebuilding his or her society.

As we just read in Zechariah 2:1–2, heaven partners with what is taking place when people's heads are lifted up. In that passage, heaven began making measurements to rebuild the city. What does this mean for us today on a practical level? I believe what takes place in this vision of Zechariah demonstrates that any resource necessary for the rebuilding of society is available in heaven—whether natural resources, financial resources, efficiency measures, Kingdom insights or relationships. The list goes on. When you and I walk as craftsmen filled with wisdom, it enables us to demonstrate the multidimensional intelligence of God, which then terrorizes demonic strongholds. That sets up the rebuilding process of our societies.

It is vital that we as believers understand the value of dedicating our lives to excellence and increasing our skills and abilities so that we can be an asset to society. That could look different for different believers, but the goal is the same—to bring the Kingdom to earth. For one person, it might look like going to school for training. For another, it might be taking the time to glean from others who are experts in their fields. It is unfortunate when believers have the heart to rebuild society but do not really possess any skills helpful in the actual rebuilding. Having the heart to contribute to society is good, but it is sharpening our skills that will make the desires of our hearts come to fruition.

No End to the Fullness of God

So far in this chapter, we have gone on quite a journey with wisdom. We have taken a look at the role of wisdom in Proverbs 8 and have seen how wisdom contributed to the creation process. We have looked at a craftsman named Bezalel in Exodus 31, who was filled with the Spirit of God in wisdom, and we have seen how that enabled him to build a tent for God exactly the way God wanted it. That led us to Zechariah 2 to see four craftsmen who were used to destroy strongholds over nations, which then led to the rebuilding of a city and a people. Now let's go to the book of Colossians and take a look at things from a New Covenant perspective.

He is the image of the invisible God, the firstborn over all creation. For by Him all things were created that are in heaven and that are on earth, visible and invisible, whether thrones or dominions or principalities or powers. All things were created through Him and for Him. And He is before all things, and in Him all things consist.

Colossians 1:15–17

A good portion of Colossians is committed to helping the readers understand Jesus Christ. We just read that all things were created through Him and for Him, that He existed before all things and that all things exist in Him. This is a buildup for verse 19, "For it pleased the Father that in Him all the fullness should dwell." This is a loaded verse in that God decided it would please Him to have all the fullness of Himself reside in His Son, Jesus. This is why we find Jesus saying in John 14:9–12 (emphasis added):

> Have I been with you so long, and yet you have not known Me, Philip? *He who has seen Me has seen the Father*; so how can you say, "Show us the Father"? Do you not believe that I am in the Father, and the Father in Me? The words that I speak to you I do not speak on My own authority; but the Father who dwells in Me does the works. *Believe Me that I am in the Father and the Father in Me*, or else believe Me for the sake of the works themselves.
>
> Most assuredly, I say to you, he who believes in Me, the works that I do he will do also; and greater works than these he will do, because I go to My Father.

Jesus was letting His disciples know that if you have seen Him, then you have also seen the Father, because all of the Father resides in Him. The fullness of God lives in His Son, Jesus. To help us understand the weight of this verse, we can look at Isaiah 9:7 (emphasis added): "Of the increase of His government and peace there will be *no end*. . . ." The phrase *no end* carries the idea that *the end does not exist.* In this verse, the government and peace of God do not have the possibility of ending at all. That is what "in Him all the fullness should dwell" in Colossians 1:19 expresses. The *fullness* of God is something we cannot fully comprehend, which should encourage us far beyond our understanding.

Now let's read again the verse that we talked about earlier in this chapter, Colossians 1:27 (NIV): "To them God has chosen to make known among the Gentiles the glorious riches of this mystery, which is Christ in you, the hope of glory." From the beginning of time, the great mystery that has been unfolding is that Christ is now in you, and He is the hope of glory. For ages, humanity has been going to a temple to find God; now *you* are that temple where God lives. This revelation of *Christ in you* and *Christ in me* opens us up to other truths and revelations that go beyond just going to heaven someday. It is a revelation about how we can demonstrate the Kingdom and its fullness here on this earth.

A company of believers all across this planet is beginning to realize that *Christ in you* means that the solutions and ideas that can remedy every problem known to man live inside them. If you do a quick study of Jesus' life and miracles, you will notice that He dealt with problems in one of five general categories: sickness and disease, finances, natural disasters, food shortages, and sin and death. Every time Jesus was confronted with a problem in one of these categories, He had a solution to offer. Not one time when a problem arose did we find Him saying, "I don't know what to do."

You will notice that most of our world's problems fit into one of these five categories. When we as the Body of Christ realize the depth and the width of what it means that Christ lives in us, then I believe we will begin to contribute in unprecedented ways to solving the complex issues that our world faces today.

Remember that you have the fullness of God living in you and that Jesus Christ wants to demonstrate this fullness through your life to the world around you. Knowing that you are a living temple for the Almighty God should make you aware that the solutions to all the complexities of life are alive in you.

When you or I run into a situation or a problem that challenges us, instead of running from it or avoiding it, let's allow the Lord to do what He does best through us—bring healing, restoration, reconciliation and answers to whatever the world faces.

3

---+---

The Light That Is in You

In the previous chapter we looked into the revelation of *Christ in you*. Let's continue that theme by talking about what another byproduct of *Christ in you* looks like. Because of its writer and its time in history, this passage of Scripture has always caught my attention: "God be merciful to us and bless us, and cause *His face to shine upon us*. Selah. *That Your way may be known on earth, Your salvation among all nations*" (Psalm 67:1–2, emphasis added). This was written during a time when people's common perception of God was, "It's best to keep at a distance, for we don't know what He is going to do." The general relationship people had with God during this era mainly involved offering Him sacrifices and living according to the many laws that would stall the punishment for sins.

Imagine that right into the middle of this culture comes King David, who carried in his heart a crazy desire to know God and know His heart. At one point David sings out,

"God, be merciful to us and bless us, and cause Your face to shine upon us so that Your ways may be known on earth."

David understood something that I do not think was common knowledge. He understood that when God shines on His people, the nations will go to God. King David's desire to know God allowed him to break free from the general way of thinking about God and tap into a Kingdom truth. In one way, I believe this is why David was called a man after God's heart. He really was after God's heart because he understood that God was after people's hearts. And he knew that if God's face shone on him, the result would be that the nations would see it and cry out, "Who's your daddy?"

Whose Is That Girl?

When my daughters were in fifth and sixth grade, my wife and I coached their basketball team. One of our key starters was my oldest daughter. She was an integral part of our team's success. Our school was small, but we had a really strong team, and we were invited to play at some of the larger school tournaments in the area. In one particular tournament, our first game was against the best sixth-grade team in town. Something happened in that game; it was as though our daughter carried the mantle of Michael Jordan and Kobe Bryant all at once. It was incredible for me to watch, both as a coach and as a dad. She seemed to make every shot she attempted, she drove the ball to the rim and she shut down the other team with her defense. All this was done against the #1 team in town.

Though we lost by two points, we were ecstatic because we had done so well against that particular team. After the game, parents and coaches from the other team, along with the referee, came to talk to me separately about how my daughter played. All of them complimented her playing skills and asked who her parents were.

I stood there proudly as a dad, saying, "She's my girl."

The referee, who also coaches a traveling team in the AAU (Amateur Athletic Union), was even recruiting her to come play for him in the spring. What happened? When my child did something amazing, the response from those who experienced it was that they wanted to find out who she was and who her daddy was.

When you and I live as true sons and daughters of the King, one of the direct side effects will be that the nations will go to Him. As the passage of Scripture that always catches my attention says, when you and I steward the influence we have that comes from the face of God shining on us, we will begin to disciple the nations in His ways. It is something David understood in his day, and it is something we must embrace for our day. Jesus is the desire of nations. David tapped into the heart of God and realized that God wants to bless us abundantly in every area of our lives, to the point that the nations take notice. I believe one of the ways for believers to disciple the nations is to walk out the favor and abundance that God shines in and on our lives.

For many people, their ability to receive favor and abundance is dependent on how much they think they deserve. If they think they only deserve a certain amount, then they will neglect or reject the favor and abundance that goes beyond what they think they deserve. This is one of the reasons your identity in Christ is crucial to your being able to receive favor. Since Christ is the absolute fullness of God and is infinite in every way, when you anchor your identity in Him, your ability to live in true abundance in mind, spirit and body becomes a reality.

Nowhere in the Bible does it give you and me permission to reject favor, blessings or abundance. We do not carry the responsibility of determining how much we are allowed to receive. That is God's responsibility. Psalm 68:19 says, "Blessed be the Lord, who daily loads us with benefits, the God of our salvation! Selah." This is why it is crucial for us as believers to confront any way of thinking that is driven by a poverty mindset. A person can have a million dollars and still live with a poverty mindset. Too often when we talk about abundance or blessings, we equate them with money. It is important not to reduce abundance and blessings simply to money. Money is only one part of all the things that make up the blessings and abundance of God.

How to Steward God's Increase

God intended His blessings to happen daily. He delights in His people. From day one, He has always taken delight in you and me. It is vital that every believer on the planet understands that God wants to pour Himself out. His nature is to move on our behalf. Revivals are often viewed as a game of Russian roulette: "Maybe this time God will move." The question should never be whether God wants to move. The question should be whether we are in a place to receive His move and steward it to a place of increase.

Look at it this way. If my marriage began with the idea that "maybe" my wife would love me after the wedding, we all know that I would act and operate completely differently than if I knew she loved me. I might find myself doing things a certain way in hopes of winning her heart. However, if I enter marriage sure of the truth that she loves me, then this becomes the premise for our relationship. Instead of living with a hope that she might love me, I will then live in such a way that I can receive her love and also deepen and strengthen my part in the relationship.

Similarly, you will live differently when you are sure that God loves you, rather than just hoping He does. The issue has never been and never will be whether God loves you. It is more about you living from a place where it is not in question whether or not God loves you—it is a certainty.

When it comes to God blessing you daily, if you do not believe He wants to bless you, and yet He does bless you, you will have a hard time realizing it is Him behind the blessings. It amazes me when I run into believers who are being promoted or blessed by God, yet they do not realize it. One of the important pieces of our discussion has to be that the "renewing of your mind" is vital to your growth as a believer. When a believer renews his or her mind, it is for the purpose of an upgrade and a promotion, not a demotion or becoming lesser.

I already talked about how we should not reduce the idea of God's abundance and blessings simply to money. It is good to realize that they should never be reduced to material things, either. But we should understand that material things ought not be neglected in the equation. Every believer on the face of the planet should be known for seeing favor and increase in every area in life—spiritually, mentally and in the physical realm. It is hard to be a resource for good if you do not have any resources. Let God bless you in every area.

It is unfortunate that a good portion of the Church looks at the Old Testament and comes to one conclusion: God was mad. When I read the Old Testament, I am continually amazed at the goodness of God as He was taking a people from the Garden of Eden through history and was showing them how to take dominion over the earth. If you look closely, you will see God walking alongside generation after generation, teaching them how to live and steward what He was putting in front of them. The advancement of humanity is directly tied to God walking alongside the generations to show us and tell us what is possible.

It is crucial that every believer understand that his or her identity has to be shaped by Christ and nothing else. When your identity is shaped apart from Christ, you are allowing yourself to be shaped by something that does not have eternity in mind. As believers, you and I need to grasp the idea that God has no end and that His government, which is love and peace, has no possibility of ceasing (see Isaiah 9:7).

When it comes to God's favor and blessing, it is important to remember that they are not directly linked to the idea that we deserve it. Often believers struggle when blessings and abundance come their way because they cannot figure out what they did to deserve it. It is typical for such believers to reject what was simply meant for them to steward to a place of increase.

The basic principle of stewardship is that God knows exactly what we can handle. I am realizing more and more that in this moment, I am in the right place at the right time in my life. I refuse to live in regret over what could have been or should have been. Since I have set my face toward Him, I trust Him more than ever. I have put all my eggs in one basket, and I live with a deep conviction that He is leading me to a place of increase. My ultimate responsibility is to steward what is in my life at this moment. This mindset puts the responsibility on me and creates ownership for what I have been given. Taking ownership of God's abundance and blessings in this way enabled the apostles to take what Jesus gave them and to see the world touched by the Gospel.

When I was a youth pastor, I remember being passionate about this topic of stewardship and looking for ways to help our junior and senior high youth grasp this biblical principle. I knew that if I could get them to grasp this, it would set them up for the long haul. I challenged them to look at what they had in their possession and steward it to a place of increase.

One of our older girls in the group often would tell us about how much she did not have in the natural or spiritual. Her poverty mindset always focused on what she lacked. After this teaching, she went home and realized that at least she had an old, rusty bike that she used to commute around town. She went to the store, bought some polish and got to work on her bike. Since it was on the old side of life, she wanted to make it look better, and she cleaned that bike up. This became a simple way of taking something in her possession and increasing it.

Some of the kids came back and shared with us how they cleaned their rooms because of this concept of stewardship. This application made a lot of parents happy. Others came back and told us about how they realized that they had been complaining about doing normal chores around the house, when really those chores were an opportunity to steward what they had been given. They ceased complaining and got busy stewarding instead, which also made some parents happy.

Jesus did not lead by doing everything for His disciples. He led by teaching and demonstrating, which set them up for success later. When He ascended back to His Father, they would then take ownership and responsibility for what they had been given. When the Lord blesses you and sets you up for success, it does not mean that you then can retire and live off that blessing for the rest of your life. In a unique way, being blessed actually creates the joyful responsibility of stewarding the blessing to a place of increase.

Find Some Shoulders to Stand On

You may be familiar with the statement, "We stand on the shoulders of those who have gone before us." In my life, I am becoming more and more aware of what is being handed to me in the form of inheritance. Desiring to know a little more about our heritage and my strong roots in the Christian faith, I interviewed one of my grandmas a few years back.

In our interview, I asked Grandma a question along the lines of, "What did your parents stand for? What were some things that they gave their life to?"

Grandma's reply was, "Prayer."

She began to tell me stories of how her parents prayed all the time. Prayer was always a part of life. No matter what was going on, they would always pray about it or pray into it.

Then I asked her, "What were some things that you and my late grandpa gave your lives to?"

She answered, "Loving people and worshiping God."

My grandparents gave their lives to loving people and living the life of worshipers. I have observed them at it up close. It is what their life was about. Even at the dinner table, we would sing in unison, "Father, we thank Thee." This was all part of their heart to worship the King as a lifestyle.

Now I look at my parents and see in them a strong love for the Holy Spirit and a determination to declare to the world that God is good. They continue to give their lives to this cause, lining up everything in their lives with the truth that God is good, so the world will see it and know it.

When I walked away from the conversation with my grandma, I realized that my strong Christian heritage is now something I take ownership of and live out in a life of prayer, worship, loving people, having a passion for the Holy Spirit and exploring the realms of the goodness of God. These are not the only things my family who went before me committed their lives to, but these are some of the key things that I now have the privilege of stewarding in my life as I "stand on their shoulders."

What is your heritage? What is your inheritance? I realize that you may be a first-generation believer, or one who for some reason does not really have any shoulders to stand on. If that is the case, you actually have a unique opportunity. What do I mean by that? Whenever I teach about spiritual inheritances or heritage, it is normal for someone to approach me and say, "I don't have as rich a heritage as you do."

My reply every time is, "That's perfect! You now have an opportunity to do something that I personally will never get to do—you get to start a heritage!"

It is an absolute privilege to start something from scratch for a generation you will never see. This is one of the most extreme opportunities that come along in stewardship—starting something from nothing. If you find yourself in the position of starting from nothing, then my advice is that you get around someone who has strong shoulders. Find someone who carries or demonstrates something in life that you desire.

One of my favorite examples of someone who did this is Kris Vallotton. Kris and his wife, Kathy, have been serving my parents in ministry for the last 35 years. They have directed their whole lives toward this purpose. Kris started out in life with a tough deck of cards. His father drowned when Kris was three, and he was raised by a single mom. Then he had a violent stepdad who instilled a foundation of fear into his life, which in turn affected how he lived and interacted with people.

In his early twenties, Kris had a total meltdown, and in his words, "was demonized." Instead of resorting to options that would take him further down that road of misery and bondage, Kris drew himself near to a man named Bill Derryberry, whose car Kris happened to be fixing one day. Bill was a real estate agent who had a heart the size of Texas, and he knew how to love people really well. Over time, Bill became a father to Kris and loved him back to mental, physical and spiritual health.

That was a long time ago, and Kris is now a father and a friend to leaders and people all over the world. He has written numerous books and is a sought-after speaker at schools and conferences. If anyone had a reason not to become successful in life, Kris is one example of such a person. Instead, he got around someone who had shoulders he could lean on for a season, and eventually he was able to stand on them. As a result, Kris's kids and grandkids have a spiritual heritage they can walk in and pass on to their kids.

Learn to Love the Dry Seasons

When I meet with people going through a tough, dry season, one of the things they will commonly say is, "I haven't heard God talk to me in a while."

I will usually ask them, "What was the last thing you remember God talking to you about?"

Their normal response is, "I don't know. It's been so long . . ."

Eventually, they will remember through the course of the conversation what it was. One person went on to say, "God was talking to me about joy and keeping a joyful heart at all times."

I asked that person, "How are you doing with keeping a joyful heart at all times?"

There was a little silence on her part as she realized that this "tough, dry season" was actually a time to learn to steward what God was teaching her.

Since God is the Master Builder and is taking you from glory to glory, it is important to remember that He is setting you up to be successful in life and to advance the Kingdom everywhere you go. The value that you place on what He says is evident in the way you navigate the tough, dry seasons—which does not mean that you sit back and relax. It means you are diligent in everything you do, and you realize that you are in the right place at the right moment at this point in your life.

It is important to remember that "this is the day the LORD has made," so let's not ruin it by complaining and grumbling. It is far better to "rejoice and be glad in it" (Psalm 118:24). Do you realize that complaining and grumbling are negative intercession? When you complain and grumble, you are interceding on behalf of the problem. You are giving it permission to stay and continue to be a problem. Instead, something must arise in you that causes you to rise above the situation so that you can defy the odds.

It is tough to expect people to change the world when they do not know how to cultivate joy at all times. "Joy" is one of the many things God will teach you. He teaches you these types of things so that you will be fully equipped to achieve success in whatever you give your life to. Remember that He knows what you can handle, so learn to steward what is in front of you. You only get into a funk when you are caught up in your own complaining, or when you are looking at something that is in front of someone else. It is time to repent from those mindsets and move into a place of expectation and hope.

Light Works Best in Dark Places

Let me point out a shift in the use of the word *light* from the Old Testament to the New Testament. Whereas in Psalm 67

David asked God to let *His face shine on him*, in Matthew 5:16 we read, "Let your light so shine before men, that they may see your good works and glorify your Father in heaven."

In the Old Testament, people were more like a reflection of God. As long you stayed in the light, you would always reflect the light that was shining. Anytime you moved out of the light, you would no longer reflect the light.

When Jesus said, "Let your light so shine," something changed. The light was no longer outside people; it was living inside them. The fruit of Christ in you is that the light shines from you. Look at it this way: Everywhere you go, the light shines. As you live and encounter the complexities of this world, your light is shining.

One thing about light is that it works the best in dark places. It is in the dark places that the power of *Christ in you* is demonstrated. The Church has always carried this revelation of the light. For the most part, it has been expressed in a mission context where the emphasis has been on unreached people groups, or it has been on trying to get people to attend church. I wholeheartedly believe these things are essential, but letting your light shine does not only mean you have to go somewhere other than where you are to let it shine. It is relevant right where you are now.

Believers need to realize that however they spend their time, whether as a CEO, a barista, a stay-at-home mom, a pro athlete or whatever they do, it is in that place that the light needs to shine. That is "true ministry."

Can you imagine if each one of us as believers approached the way we spend our time with the idea in mind that everything we do in life is ministry unto the King? We would have fewer believers trying to get into the pulpits to preach and a lot more believers spending more of their time touching the people they live with and interact with every day. The result would be Kingdom demonstrations and manifestations that we did not even know could exist, and the Kingdom would advance in ways we did not know were possible.

One of the subtle shifts taking place in the Body of Christ involves the emphasis on evangelism. This is a delicate topic, and I have no intention of minimizing evangelism or shrinking from the emphasis on souls getting saved, which is carrying out the Great Commission. It is important, though, to ask questions about our methods. The message is sacred; the method is not.

Often in our attempts to lead souls to Jesus, we have forgotten that these are *people* we are talking about. Sometimes we talk about souls who need saving as if they are objects or numbers. There is an underlying belief in the Body of Christ that if you are not leading someone to Christ, then you are not doing evangelism. This has pressured many into a form of forced evangelism.

Let's not forget Jesus' approach. He went about "doing good." He was adding benefit to the world and the people around Him. Scripture gives us numerous examples of how He did it. At a party, He helped the host with a shortage of wine by making more. One time the disciples' business was suffering as they labored all night and caught no fish, and Jesus came up and advised them to cast their nets on the other side. This was great business advice, and they ended up reaping an abundance of fish. Jesus played with children and often referred to them as the ones who understood the Kingdom. His ministry did not largely revolve around altar calls, but around a lifestyle of loving the world around Him. And in the process, people believed and came into the Kingdom.

When you let your light shine, you will begin to see justice happen where there is injustice, healing take place where there is sickness, prosperity come where there is poverty. Souls (people) will get saved, businesses will thrive and society will be governed by the power of love, not fear. All this and more is the result of letting your light shine. It is similar to being in a dark room and turning on a light. It seems as if the moment a light shines in a dark place, people begin to move toward it. The same thing happens in the spiritual. Light wins every time.

Light Attracts the Nations

One of the reasons King Solomon became a wise man was that his father, King David, taught him the ways of kings while Solomon was still a little boy. In many ways, Solomon lived out the revelation that his father had received. This example is one of the rare places in history where you see a generation increase what was given to them.

Look at the story of how King Solomon interacted with the Queen of Sheba. This story is one of the fruits of the revelation that came about as a result of God's light shining on and reflecting off Solomon (see again Psalm 67:1–2). As you read the story, you will see that the queen was observing everything about Solomon, from the way he offered sacrifices to the way his servants were dressed. Overwhelmed, she was in awe of what she saw and experienced. One of the things the queen did was ask Solomon some hard questions, but nothing was too hard for him to answer. The queen's actions illustrate that it is the desire of nations to find truth and the answers to the problems they face.

> When the queen of Sheba heard about the fame of Solomon and his relationship to the LORD, she came to test Solomon with hard questions. Arriving at Jerusalem with a very great caravan—with camels carrying spices, large quantities of

gold, and precious stones—she came to Solomon and talked with him about all that she had on her mind. Solomon answered all her questions; nothing was too hard for the king to explain to her. When the queen of Sheba saw all the wisdom of Solomon and the palace he had built, the food on his table, the seating of his officials, the attending servants in their robes, his cupbearers, and the burnt offerings he made at the temple of the LORD, she was overwhelmed.

She said to the king, "The report I heard in my own country about your achievements and your wisdom is true. But I did not believe these things until I came and saw with my own eyes. Indeed, not even half was told me; in wisdom and wealth you have far exceeded the report I heard. How happy your people must be! How happy your officials, who continually stand before you and hear your wisdom! Praise be to the LORD your God, who has delighted in you and placed you on the throne of Israel. Because of the LORD's eternal love for Israel, he has made you king to maintain justice and righteousness."

And she gave the king 120 talents of gold, large quantities of spices, and precious stones. Never again were so many spices brought in as those the queen of Sheba gave to King Solomon.

(Hiram's ships brought gold from Ophir; and from there they brought great cargoes of almugwood and precious stones. The king used the almugwood to make supports for the temple of the LORD and for the royal palace, and to make harps and lyres for the musicians. So much almugwood has never been imported or seen since that day.)

King Solomon gave the queen of Sheba all she desired and asked for, besides what he had given her out of his royal bounty. Then she left and returned with her retinue to her own country.

1 Kings 10:1–13 NIV

This is a very early example of what needs to become commonplace for every believer. Because Christ is in you and His wisdom resides in you, you will stand before people from all walks of life—your neighbor, the soccer coach, city leaders, perhaps even kings and queens—and they will present hard questions to you about things they are facing. You will be able to answer them with the wisdom that lives in you, because of Christ in you.

Are you asking yourself the question, *How do I get that kind of wisdom?* First Kings 3:5–15 shows us what Solomon did:

> At Gibeon the LORD appeared to Solomon in a dream by night; and God said, "Ask! What shall I give you?"
>
> And Solomon said: "You have shown great mercy to Your servant David my father, because he walked before You in truth, in righteousness, and in uprightness of heart with You; You have continued this great kindness for him, and You have given him a son to sit on his throne, as it is this day. Now, O LORD my God, You have made Your servant king instead of my father David, but I am a little child; I do not know how to go out or come in. And Your servant is in the midst of Your people whom You have chosen, a great people, too numerous to be numbered or counted. Therefore give to Your servant an understanding heart to judge Your people, that I may discern between good and evil. For who is able to judge this great people of Yours?"
>
> The speech pleased the Lord, that Solomon had asked this thing. Then God said to him: "Because you have asked this thing, and have not asked long life for yourself, nor have asked riches for yourself, nor have asked the life of your enemies, but have asked for yourself understanding to discern justice, behold, I have done according to your words; see, I have given you a wise and understanding heart, so that there has not been anyone like you before you, nor shall any like you arise after you. And I have also given you what you have not asked: both riches and honor, so that there shall not be

anyone like you among the kings all your days. So if you walk in My ways, to keep My statutes and My commandments, as your father David walked, then I will lengthen your days."

Then Solomon awoke; and indeed it had been a dream. And he came to Jerusalem and stood before the ark of the covenant of the LORD, offered up burnt offerings, offered peace offerings, and made a feast for all his servants.

God appeared to Solomon in a dream, and his response to God's question was, "God, give me wisdom and understanding."

This made God happy, so much so that His reply was, "Since you asked for wisdom, I will give you everything your heart desires."

In 1989, my parents put together a birthday party to celebrate my thirteenth birthday at our home on East Branch Road in Weaverville, California. I remember that day clearly. As my family and friends were singing "Happy Birthday" and I was getting ready to blow out the candles, someone said, "Make a wish."

As I was blowing out the candles, my wish was, "God, I ask for wisdom." Ever since that day, I have continued to ask Him for more wisdom. This has been a major theme in my life from a young age, and it will continue to be a theme.

One of our chief responsibilities in life is to serve the people around us. As you are reading this, people all over the world are discussing problems and issues they are facing and digging for solutions. Meetings and summits are being held largely for the purpose of eradicating diseases or social issues that are decimating populations around the world. There are countries on the verge of war and leaders pondering whether the next step is war or diplomacy. Closer to home, city leaders are looking for solutions to the violence and crime that run rampant on our streets.

Perhaps you are the one trying to find the solution or answers to some really deep issues. The revelation of *Christ in you* carries the power to unravel the greatest mysteries and challenges that our generation faces today. This is why it is vital that those of us in the Body of Christ realize who lives in us and what that means. It means far more for us and for those around us than just having a "ticket" to heaven.

Christ is in you so that the light can shine where it is desired and needed. It is time to trust the light that is in you and know that it works! Remember that light works best in the dark situations and dark places. And remember that since Christ lives in you and His light shines out from you, you can walk with confidence, realizing that you carry the solution to whatever problems cross your path.

4

— + —

Kingdom Now
or Kingdom Later?

Occasionally I am asked this question: "Is the Kingdom now, or is it later?" This question is usually birthed by a desire to understand why we see the reality of some of the things the Bible promises, but we do not see other things it promises. In our journey through life, we do see God break through into our realm, but we also seemingly face the reality of defeat.

We find ourselves straddling the chasm between victory and seeming defeat all the time. We see how one person's life is saved through the healing of a terminal disease, while another person's life is ravished by the same unhealed disease, so the person dies. We see miracles in marriages, finances and relationships for some people, but then we do not see miracles for other people in the same areas. When you choose to live a lifestyle of faith and you expect the supernatural to take place, this question of Kingdom now or Kingdom later percolates to the surface in these situations.

77

The posture we take about this question as believers is key to how successfully we will navigate through the tough issues we face. I have had the privilege of being in an environment most of my life where I see firsthand what it looks like to contend for breakthrough in seeing miracles, signs and wonders. When I look back, I can easily see how we at Bethel Church got where we are today, as well as seeing hints about where we are headed. There seem to have been certain moments in our journey when, faced with large hurdles, we decided to contend for breakthrough regardless of how we felt or thought. It was in those times that we saw an increase of breakthrough. Somehow, our decision to "jump the hurdle" with a no-matter-what attitude led us to live in a place of greater authority. There is a great level of mystery in this process.

About a decade ago, my Grandpa Johnson was diagnosed with cancer. It was a huge blow to us as a family. We faced a seven-month battle during which Grandpa and our whole family contended for a miracle for his life. As time went by, he became sicker and sicker. In the last week of his life, 25 of us as a family camped out at my grandparents' house. We took turns taking care of Grandpa and tending to his needs. Every evening we would all cram into his room and surround his bed, and we would worship and pray for hours. During all this, we knew there were thousands of people around the world praying for his miracle, and we could feel the prayers of the saints.

It was one of the most mystery-filled weeks of our lives. In the midst of the sickness, pain and suffering, we experienced a part of heaven that was unreal. During that time, we received words and promises about his healing and held them up earnestly. Never once did we blame God for the situation, but rather we partnered with Him to see healing come. We had notable prophets call and give us words about what was happening. I personally felt that the Lord told me Grandpa had twenty more years to live, so that became my prayer and declaration.

As Grandpa's final week went by, there was no improvement. One of the words that we had received from a prophet was that this journey was going to give us more authority and power over cancer. We knew that in the mystery of it all, cancer was in trouble.

Late one night, Grandpa passed away. For me, this outcome was confusing and painful all at once. I could not reconcile it with what I thought I had heard—that he would live another twenty years. Yet though the outcome was completely different from what I had hoped and prayed for, I had a deep sense that something good and important was going to come out of it all.

The very next morning, just a few hours after Grandpa's passing, all the family (which now numbered 32 present) gathered in my grandparents' living room to hold a family meeting. The agenda of the meeting was centered on affirming the truth that God is good and that we would never change the subject when it comes to signs, wonders and miracles. We would never look at sickness the same way, and we would continue to contend for healing no matter what. At one point, we all looked each other in the eye and made a commitment not to back down from this. This was important for us as a family, because it is in moments of pain and confusion that it is easy to come to a conclusion outside of the truth.

This scenario took place a decade ago. Looking back on that moment and seeing what has happened in our personal family life and church family life, we can see that there has been a dramatic increase in miracles altogether, especially in the area of cancer. A seeming defeat brought us new resolve to press on into victory. I retell this story here not for the purpose of creating a theology or trying to figure out the mystery of it all, but to place a resolve in your heart not to deter from the course that you are called to as a believer—to see the Kingdom come on this earth as it is in heaven.

The Room with an Instrument

One of the keys to understanding the Kingdom is to get hold of the heart of God about who He is and what He intends to do in the ages to come. Look at Isaiah 9:7 (emphasis added):

> Of the increase of His government and peace
> *There will be no end,*
> Upon the throne of David and over His kingdom,
> To order it and establish it with judgment and justice
> From that time forward, even forever.
> *The zeal of the* LORD *of hosts will perform this.*

Isaiah is prophesying about the coming of the Messiah and the government that will follow His coming. One of the phrases Isaiah uses is that His government will have no end. That communicates the idea that an "end" does not even exist. The "end" is not an option or even a possibility. This can be tough for us to grasp since we live in the realm of time, surrounded by things that have a beginning and an end. The concept of something not ending is beyond our natural comprehension, but it is understandable through our spiritual comprehension. It is important as sons and daughters of the King that we learn to be guided and steered by a Kingdom that has no end in sight. It will change the way we live, how we think and what we expect.

Let me use an illustration to help us understand this idea that the Kingdom has no end. Let's say the Kingdom of God is a very large room. This large room has a door that separates what is inside the Kingdom and what is outside the Kingdom. Outside this room is the kingdom of darkness, where you and I lived before we gave our lives to the Lord. The moment we confessed our sins and asked Him to be our Savior, the door to the Kingdom was opened to us. Now, through the grace of God, we are in the middle of this large room.

Since the Kingdom of God has no end, when I entered I noticed the room is expansive. It has a depth to it I have never seen anywhere before. As I look around I notice what occupies the room, but I cannot yet give you much detail about it. It will not be until I actually engage with what I see and become familiar with it that I will be able to fill you in on the details.

Off in the distance, I notice a piano. If someone asks me what I see, I can say I see a piano, but that does not mean I know how to play it. This is where I see believers become confused by the idea of having access versus having authority. It is important to know the difference between seeing something in the Kingdom and being able to "play" it. When you see something in the Kingdom, it means you can have it if you want it. In Ephesians 1–3, Paul spends quite a bit of time telling his readers about the greatness and fullness of what is available to the believer. We can have as much of the Kingdom as we want; it really is up to us.

To continue the illustration, let's say I walk over to the piano, but I have had no prior experience with it. I have been given access to the piano, but it is my responsibility to engage with it and learn to play it. As I sit there and press the piano keys, there is a good chance that I will play poorly. Awkward sounds, along with bad notes, will come out of it because I have never played it before. I need some time to practice and learn more about the piano before I can make beautiful music.

This process is completely normal and obvious when we think of it in relation to playing a musical instrument, but in spiritual applications, it is a concept often misunderstood in the Church. We need to learn to create church cultures where people who are experiencing aspects of the Kingdom for the first time can receive grace and space to practice on the piano for a while, so to speak. We need to allow them time to learn, and then to process and practice what they are learning.

When I was teaching my daughters how to ride a bike, do you think I got upset when they fell or did not get it quite right at the start? No, of course not. When they fell, it propelled me to make sure they were okay and then to help them learn even more about riding a bike. Likewise, the day you got saved and became a Christian, it did not mean that you suddenly knew how to do everything believers have access to doing. It meant that you were enabled with grace to learn and experience the Kingdom in a way that had been impossible for you before you were saved.

When we do not know how to play the piano right away, spiritually speaking, it is common for us to walk away from it and announce, "It's not for now, but for another day." Whatever the "piano" represents, we decide it must be a "Kingdom later" kind of thing, and we take the responsibility off ourselves and put it back on God, as if it were His fault that we do not know how to play the piano. When you and I are exposed to an aspect of the Kingdom, for example miracles, and we do not see them happening in our life, too often we say, "They're not for today; they're for another time." Yet it is crucial that we understand this truth: When we see something in the Kingdom, we can have it.

Here at Bethel, it is commonplace to hear of a miracle, healing or prophetic word being given to someone. We joke that "our people prophesy over anything that moves." What some people do not realize is that this type of environment did not come overnight. There is a deep, rich history of individuals who made a decision at some point to go after healing and miracles and "not to change the subject" in these areas. They refused to leave the piano; they remained on that stool and continued to press the keys until what was coming out began to sound like music. They began to learn simple pieces of music, and went on learning, all the way to mastering complex pieces. As they played, the nations began to hear the song. As a result, many have sold everything because they wanted to be part of our community of believers so that they, too, can learn to "play the piano."

I often wonder how many of us have walked away from the piano, spiritually speaking, too soon. Every believer needs to live with the conviction of the reality of the Kingdom *now*. We need to know that since we are children of a good Dad, when we see something, we can possess it. The zeal of the Lord is such a force that it will ensure that the coming of the Kingdom happens. We *can* learn to play—there is not much we can do to stop it, avoid it or even miss it. The zeal of God is driven by a jealousy to see His Kingdom come.

From Glory to Glory

Understanding how things work in the Kingdom is essential. I often encounter believers who are frustrated and constantly spinning their wheels when it comes to living a lifestyle that mimics the Kingdom of God. We have to realize that there is only one direction in the Kingdom—from glory to glory. There is no other direction. Second Corinthians 3:16–18 tells us so:

> Nevertheless when one turns to the Lord, the veil is taken away.
> Now the Lord is the Spirit; and where the Spirit of the Lord

is, there is liberty. But we all, with unveiled face, beholding as in a mirror the glory of the Lord, are being transformed into the same image from glory to glory, just as by the Spirit of the Lord.

This passage is profound in so many ways. The truth it releases is this: When you set your face toward God, you are then put on a journey of going only one direction in the Kingdom, from glory to glory. Too often we think the opposite—that we are going backward. At this point in my life, I am realizing that my responsibility is to keep my face set on Him. If I do that, He takes care of the rest.

You may ask, "What about all the sins I've committed or all the wrong things I've done?" The key to grasping this idea of "glory to glory" is that when you turn your face to Him, it is in that turning, which is repentance, that the Holy Spirit releases liberty. He removes the veil over your eyes, which allows you to see His glory. Seeing His glory begins to transform you into His glory.

The relevance of the truth "where the Spirit is, there is liberty" is paramount to our walking out the Kingdom lifestyle. The role liberty plays in our lives is larger than most of us make it out to be. One of the ways God raises up people is by giving them the choice *not* to be bound by their past, their surroundings and whatever is going on internally. Living in liberty in the Lord is going from glory to glory.

Have you noticed that when a child sees a stairway, he or she wants to go up the stairs? I have yet to see a child turn down the opportunity. Why? It is built into the way children are designed to do life—forward and upward. It is something I believe we are born with. One reason children are so quick to tell you what they want to be when they grow up is that instinctively, they do not allow anything to tell them they cannot do something. That is the way it is with you and me as God's kids. When we live in the King's house, our understanding and our abilities are according to the measure of the abundance of the King.

Desperation versus Hunger

Since we live in the abundance of the King, I have never understood why people are desperate toward a good God. By that I mean they constantly express their awareness of lack and focus on what they do not have, when all the time, as children of the King, they have access to the One who has limitless resources. I remember even as a young boy watching some people cry out to God in desperation over and over for many years. They seemed to get more discouraged and depressed as time went on. It never made sense to me. If God is good, why are we so desperate toward Him?

It would make complete sense to be desperate toward an angry God, if that is your image of Him. This may be why we see so many people spend their lives being desperate toward God. Their paradigm is built around the idea that God is angry. When you are dealing with an angry leader, the way you get anything from him or her is to find a way to lower and possibly humiliate yourself. Angry leaders feel powerful when the people below them approach them in such a way, and they like having the power to control the outcome of a subordinate's situation.

But we do not have an angry God we need to be desperate toward. If I had to be desperate about spending time with my wife, would you call that a healthy marriage? No. Then why do we glorify the act of desperation in our walk with God? Essentially, it is an inferior form of relationship. Unfortunately, this is a common approach to God for many believers today.

Desperation is a dysfunction that needs to be purged from any Kingdom-minded person. It is tough to experience the vastness of the Kingdom when we are desperate. When we act desperate for the things we already have access to, we are choosing to live in a state of unbelief.

Whenever I teach on this topic, whatever the setting, almost without fail someone will approach me and admit that he or she struggles to break out of a lifestyle of desperation. Desperation is based on the awareness of lack. Hunger is based on the awareness of abundance. If we truly believe we are living in the Kingdom and that the things of the Kingdom are within our reach, then it is time to move out of desperation and into hunger. We must move in this direction.

If you were to ask me if I am ever desperate in the prayers and longings of my life, my answer would be yes. However, desperation is not the basis of my relationship with God. It is important not to let desperation become the cornerstone of our relationship with God. The life, ministry and teachings of Jesus revealed the goodness of God, and that is what our cornerstone should be. When God's goodness becomes your cornerstone, your paradigm shifts and you realize you have access to all the abundance He offers.

Get Your Own Milk

One of the keys to growing in confidence and authority in the things of the Kingdom can be found in Matthew 6 and Luke 18. Let's first take a look at Matthew 6:5–8:

> And when you pray, you shall not be like the hypocrites. For they love to pray standing in the synagogues and on the corners of the streets, that they may be seen by men. Assuredly, I say to you, they have their reward. But you, when you pray,

go into your room, and when you have shut your door, pray to your Father who is in the secret place; and your Father who sees in secret will reward you openly. And when you pray, do not use vain repetitions as the heathen do. For they think that they will be heard for their many words.
Therefore do not be like them. For your Father knows the things you have need of before you ask Him.

A number of years ago as I was reading this passage, I was incredibly moved, especially by this statement: "Therefore do not be like them. For your Father knows the things you have need of before you ask Him" (verse 8). Jesus is teaching His disciples about prayer, and He is also showing them a Kingdom principle that needs to be an integral part of our foundation. He was revealing the nature of God when it comes to life in general and the things that you need. When it comes to things that you need, Jesus makes it really clear that there is no need to ask, because God, being a good Father, knows how to take care of His children.

This is one of the super important things we must embrace about the Kingdom. It is more than just a theory. God knows what we need. Many believers go through countless religious rituals based on a belief that God does not know how to take care of His children. But this idea that God knows how to take care of us is one of the key building blocks in your growth as a believer. I exhort you to make this a foundation that you build your life on. It is essential to every aspect of your personal life, your family life and the way you touch and interact with other people.

I believe one of the essential master keys to the Kingdom that every believer should have in his or her possession is simply, "I am the child of a really good Dad." If believers carried this key confidently in their hands, I do believe we would see the Body of Christ emerge in ways unprecedented in history. Imagine with me if the Body of Christ at large were living from the certainty of *being* loved by God, not *trying* to be loved by God? The immediate impact it would have in believers' lives and in the world around them would be hard to quantify because it would produce so much life in cities and nations. Fear would be eradicated from our society. People would not fill their desire to be loved with the vices of this world; they would be loved from the Source of all love. The social statistics in our society would have to be measured with a whole new set of criteria. The way we live would forever be altered. People would find their hearts charged with courage and strength to do the impossible. The ongoing conversation people have of finding the one idea that could change everything would be over, because *this idea is it*—the idea that the foundation of the Kingdom is built on love.

Now let's look at Luke 18:1–8:

> Then He spoke a parable to them, that men always ought to pray and not lose heart, saying: "There was in a certain city a judge who did not fear God nor regard man. Now there was a widow in that city; and she came to him, saying, 'Get justice for me from my adversary.' And he would not for a while; but afterward he said within himself, 'Though I do not fear God nor regard man, yet because this widow troubles me I will avenge her, lest by her continual coming she weary me.'"
>
> Then the Lord said, "Hear what the unjust judge said. And shall God not avenge His own elect who cry out day and night to Him, though He bears long with them? I tell you that He will avenge them speedily. Nevertheless, when the Son of Man comes, will He really find faith on the earth?"

When my daughters were born, they did what every baby is expert at: They cried whenever they needed something, whether they were hungry, needed a diaper change or just were not happy. As parents, Candace and I always responded to the cries of our children. It was natural; no one told us to do it. It is what parents do. When we tended to their cries, we would try to figure out what they needed.

As they reached around the age of two, we started to teach them that when they needed something, instead of crying they could communicate with words. We would tell them in their moment of need, "You don't need to cry; just use your words." What were we doing? We were letting them know there was another way to go about things.

When they reached the age of three or four, we took all the plastic cups out of the upper cupboards and put them in a cupboard down low, where the girls could reach for a cup by themselves. Whenever they asked for milk, we would tell them, "Go get a cup, and we'll get the milk." Then we would meet them in the middle of the kitchen, and we would pour the milk into the cup they had gotten on their own. What were we doing? We were co-laboring together to accomplish something.

Now my daughters are in junior high, and they never ask us anymore if they can get a glass of milk. Why? They have the authority and ability to get it themselves. Over time, we taught them that they do not need to cry out to get what they need, because they have gained the ability and authority to take care of it themselves.

What always amazes me is that God the Father's grace is so big that He will allow us to cry out continually to Him, and just as He said in Luke 18:8, He will answer speedily. But at the same time, in the same verse, the last statement Jesus makes is, "When I come back, will I find faith on the earth?" Jesus is looking for a person who will learn to move in faith. He is looking for a person who will move mountains, not just cry out that the mountains would move.

Faith is essential in our walk with God, not only for our salvation, but also for demonstrating His goodness on the earth. Whenever we have a breakthrough in our lives, it should move us to a place of authority in that area. I am diligent in my pursuit of breakthrough, whether it be in the area of provision, healing or restoration. Every breakthrough becomes ground that I stand on for the rest of my life. Crying out for the same thing over and over is not the goal or the plan of God for us. Rather, His plan is for us to move into a realm of faith and authority.

Before we move on to the next chapter, I want you to ask yourself some questions to help you apply and assimilate what we just talked about. First, ask yourself,

- Do I view God as an angry God?

If you answered yes to this question and you desire to view God as a good Father, then it is time to invite the Holy Spirit to show you why you view God as angry. This will begin a journey of freedom that will help expose lies or ideas that you thought were true, but were not. It will lead you to a place where you no longer see your Father as an angry God.

The next questions you want to ask yourself are these:

- What are some things or some areas that I have seen in the Kingdom but have not done my part to access and take authority in?
- How can I sit down at the spiritual "piano" and learn to play the instrument (so to speak)?

Once you have identified at least one area, it is time to aim your efforts and energy toward it. For example, let's say the area you identify is having the "joy of the Lord." If I were you, I would set out on a journey to learn what the joy of the Lord is by studying in the Bible what it says about joy. Ask the Lord to show you His joy and to help you find people who walk in that joy. When you do this, it will expose any lies or belief systems that hinder joy from emerging in your life. There is a tremendous amount of strength in the joy of the Lord (see Nehemiah 8:10).

Here are two more questions I want you to ask yourself:

- Is my relationship with God based on what my needs are?
- Am I still crying out to God for everything in life?

If you answered yes to these questions, then your next step would be to ask yourself this question:

- Why don't I trust God to take care of my needs?

These questions can seem difficult, but asking them will start a beautiful process in you. They will begin to help you see where these negative thoughts come from so you can replace them with what is true. As you think through and answer these questions, I encourage you to invite the Holy Spirit to reveal both the problems in your thinking and the solutions to you. The Holy Spirit will also help you in the process as you move from your old foundations to a new one—the foundation of the goodness of God. The light at the end of this tunnel is freedom in Christ, so let's keep running toward the light. After all, the light of the Kingdom is not just for later; it is for *now*.

5

Conviction—The Birthplace of Confidence

Arrogance is driven by what it can gain. Confidence is motivated by what it can give. And confidence is birthed out of our convictions, those things we believe in so deeply that nothing can shake us no matter what comes our way.

One of the major advantages of living in our times is that we have incredible access to literature and to audio and video files filled with our history. We can learn so much about the lives of people who wrote the story of our past. Some of my favorite books are biographies, which fascinate me because I like reading about how different people essentially helped direct the course of human history. Whether their contribution involved some grand idea, some new invention or some great innovation, one thing I have observed is that each of the men and women who changed the course of history had an extremely deep conviction about what he or she believed in. In many ways, you could not separate them from their convictions.

One thing all great people have in common is that they would pay any price for what they believe in. No comfort in the world is enticing enough to pull them away from their convictions. No earthly possession has the power to keep them from pursuing the impossible. In many ways, they become possessed and obsessed with whatever it is they believe in. This character trait is essential for anyone who desires to affect the course of human history. If our convictions do not fully possess us, then at some point when the pressure is too much or the critics are too loud or the pain is too unbearable, we will retract.

Throughout history, you see men and women giving themselves wholly and completely to the cause or dream that burned inside them. Think of men like William Wilberforce, who gave himself to ending slavery. Twenty-six years went by between the passing of the Slave Trade Act of 1807, which many hoped would end slavery in the British Empire, and the Slavery Abolition Act of 1833, which actually did abolish slavery there. Having spent all those years totally dedicated to the cause, Wilberforce died three days after this bill passed.[1]

Amelia Earhart's life was shaped by her relentless pursuit of her passion to fly. She was the first woman to fly solo across the Atlantic in 1932. Her love for flying ended up costing Earhart her life; she disappeared attempting to fly across the Pacific Ocean.

Martin Luther King Jr. gave his entire life to the civil rights movement in the mid-1900s. He became a voice for a generation of people who had no voice. He lived with deep conviction in his dream that people from all races and all backgrounds could live in harmony and peace. The dream

---

1. Eric Metaxas, *Seven Men: And the Secret of Their Greatness* (Nashville: Thomas Nelson, 2013), 55.

he carried essentially led our nation toward radical change and exposed a major evil underlying our society—racism—that needed to be purged from our way of life. His dream, too, ended up costing him his life. Yet even today, most of us still feel strongly convicted about the vital importance of his dream as we move closer to its realization.

These are only a few of the many people who lived with a deep conviction that touched every part of their being. No one is willing to die for something they do not fully or completely believe in, but for those with a deep conviction about something, no sacrifice is too great. As we look at the lives and ministries of Jesus and His disciples, we see that they lived lives full of conviction, confidence and boldness. At one point some of them got in trouble for being so bold, yet they prayed that they would be given even more boldness, whatever the price.

When I read stories of the great men and women in Scripture, I notice a common denominator among them. The men and women who defied reason by going against the status quo and doing what they were told they could not do all had a deep conviction of who God is and who they were in His equation. Some of them grasped it right away, and others came to understand it over time. Nonetheless, because they had such a clear and deep conviction of who God is and the part He had for them to play in His Kingdom, it birthed a confidence in them to move forward and accomplish the great feats of old that we still read about with such fascination today.

The Intent of Grace

In our journey toward learning to walk in confidence, it is important that we understand the full intent of grace. Grace was not given so we would live in a place of guilt; it was given so we could move out of guilt and step into what God has for us. In my experience, most Christians believe the latter, yet seem to struggle walking it out. If we believe grace was given based on our need, then we will live in a constant tug-of-war. But if we understand that grace was given so we could live in a place of full access to God's abundance, then we will start experiencing measures of the Kingdom that so far, we have only dreamed about.

It is so important for us to understand the intent of grace. One of my desires is to help people move and live in the realm of grace. I am troubled when I see people living in a place of guilt, yet saying they live in grace. Think about how often believers use the statement "I'm a sinner saved by grace." This has become the anthem of many Christians, who use it to help themselves stay humble and to explain their shortcomings to themselves and others. But I do not think the intent of grace was for us to continue identifying ourselves as sinners.

The apostle Paul wrote in one of his letters to Timothy, "This is a faithful saying and worthy of all acceptance, that Christ Jesus came into the world to save sinners, of whom I am chief" (1 Timothy 1:15). This verse is often misunderstood and taken out of context. We read it as though Paul is letting Timothy know of his current state as "chief sinner." It is better understood, however, in the larger context of what Paul is communicating to Timothy in the verses that precede it:

> But we know that the law is good if one uses it lawfully, knowing this: *that the law is not made for a righteous person*, but for the lawless and insubordinate, for the ungodly and for sinners, for the unholy and profane, for murderers of fathers and murderers of mothers, for manslayers, for fornicators, for sodomites, for kidnappers, for liars, for perjurers, and if

there is any other thing that is contrary to sound doctrine, according to the glorious gospel of the blessed God which was committed to my trust.

And I thank Christ Jesus our Lord who has enabled me, because He counted me faithful, putting me into the ministry, although *I was formerly* a blasphemer, a persecutor, and an insolent man; but *I obtained mercy* because I did it ignorantly in unbelief.

1 Timothy 1:8–13, emphasis added

Paul is well-known for his letters and teachings about righteousness obtained through faith in Christ. In verses 9–10 in this passage, he makes the connection that the law is for sinners, not for the righteous. He was a major advocate of the conviction that we died with Christ, but have also risen with Him (see Romans 6:8).

If all this is true, why do we assert that Paul is stating he is still a sinner, and in fact, chief among them? I believe what Paul is saying is, "I *was* a chief sinner, but because of Christ's death and resurrection, I am now a righteous person through Him." In verse 13 he says that he was "formerly" some sinful things, which implies that such was no longer his identity after Christ. He was drawing a line in his life and showing that the mercy of God brought him out of sin and into the righteousness of God.

It is important that we as believers understand that being a sinner is something we formerly *were*, but currently *are not*. We have a new Master, and His name is not "sin." His name is Jesus. The importance of delineating when you were a sinner and when you became a righteous person is vital—it reflects who your Master is. Romans 6:1–6 reads,

What shall we say then? Shall we continue in sin that grace may abound? Certainly not! How shall we who died to sin live any longer in it? Or do you not know that as many of us as were baptized into Christ Jesus were baptized into His death? Therefore we were buried with Him through baptism into death, that just as Christ was raised from the dead by the glory of the Father, even so we also should walk in newness of life.

For if we have been united together in the likeness of His death, certainly we also shall be in the likeness of His resurrection, knowing this, that our old man was crucified with Him, that the body of sin might be done away with, that we should no longer be slaves of sin.

Jesus did not die for your sins so that you could still identify yourself as a sinner. He paid the ultimate price so that you could be called the righteousness of God. After you turned your face to God, you were grafted into His bloodline and became His son or daughter. So rather than saying, "I'm a sinner saved by grace," a more accurate statement would be to say something like this: "I was a sinner, and grace is what has transformed me into a saint."

Here are some important questions we need to ask ourselves: *What is the intent of grace? Is grace just meant to get me into heaven? Or is grace meant to help me be like Christ?*

As we begin to understand the intent of grace, we begin to move in the direction of grace. Let's take a look at what grace was intended for, starting at John 3:16: "For God so loved the world that he gave his one and only Son, that whoever believes in him shall not perish but have eternal life." God sent His Son, Jesus, to die on the cross and be resurrected into a perfect, glorified state. This was done so that none would perish, but would have eternal life. Grace and guilt are not friends; they do not know how to coexist together. The grace God extended to every person is not given so we will feel extra guilty for what we have done or are doing. It is meant to bring us to conviction, after which repentance brings us to freedom and authority.

In my experience, it is common for believers to say that they believe in the grace of God, but then only step into it partially. Unfortunately, many measure the amount of grace they receive by determining how much they *think* they deserve. If this were the case, then we could boast in how much grace we have earned (see Ephesians 2:8–9), but actually, what you think you deserve has nothing to do with how much grace you receive. Grace was meant to surpass our need and bring us into a continual place of abundance. Grace is not only sufficient for our debt. In more ways than not, it is designed to take us into realms of abundance that allow us to live from a place of resource and authority. You do not have much authority when you have nothing to give, but grace brings all the abundance we need.

Colossians 1:1–2 reads, "Paul, an apostle of Jesus Christ by the will of God, and Timothy our brother, *to the saints* and faithful brethren in Christ who are in Colosse: Grace to you and peace from God our Father and the Lord Jesus Christ" (emphasis added). In verse 2, Paul makes it really clear whom he is addressing in this letter—it is written "to the saints." It is important to know that when we read Paul's letter, we are reading what Paul wrote to a group of believers, and in some cases, to a group of churches.

I remember God telling me in 1996 to pay attention to the opening sections in Paul's letters. I often would read right over them to get to the "meat" of his books, but you can miss a lot that way. It came to me while paying attention to Paul's openers that he desires his readers to grasp the idea that they are "saints" and not sinners. When we recognize whom Paul was writing to, we will better grasp the intent of his letters.

Paul lived in an extremely pivotal time in history. With the death and resurrection of Jesus, humanity moved from a law-based paradigm to a grace-based paradigm. Paul carried the responsibility and revelation of helping the early Church move out of a sinner mentality into a saint mentality. This proved quite a task. Paul gave his entire life to this one cause: unraveling the greatest mystery of all time, "Christ in you." He was leading the early Church toward understanding that they were no longer required to live from the outside in, but to live from the inside out. Paul paid an incredible price for helping usher in that considerable paradigm shift.

Knowing the importance of this one word, *saint*, is integral to our grasping the rest of Paul's letter to the Colossians. As saints, we live as a righteous people. Because of the cross and resurrection of Jesus, we have been acquitted of every charge brought against us. This is the grace of God, who extends mercy to you and me. How we understand His grace will determine how we embrace what He teaches us. The saint mindset lives in such a way that it embraces the promises of God for the present—now—and lives *from* the promise and not *to* the promise.

The goal of every believer is to be aware of God's promises and live with them in his or her possession. It is unfortunate that some believers are aware of His promises, yet live only hoping that one day they will taste of them. The sinner mindset tends to put the blessings and promises of God into another day, and it easily embraces the worst for the present.

People who still have a sinner mindset will read the blessings and promises in the Bible as a far-off goal. They will create a list of things they have to do before they get the blessings and promises, and working through that list will become a religious process in their lives. But remember that it is God's goodness that leads us to repentance (see Romans 2:4). If our actions could get us more of His goodness, then we would create cultures in which we would boast of who has done the most to get the most. God loves to reveal Himself to us, and it is upon this revelation that we realize we need to repent. Then it becomes clear which things in our lives we need to walk away from because they are not good.

In order to fully grasp what God has in store for you, it is paramount to understand that you are a saint, *now*! The moment you understand that, you are ready to experience the intent of grace—that when you surrender your life to Him, you are a saint and have full access to the Kingdom. Paul states in Ephesians 1, "Blessed be the God and Father of our Lord Jesus Christ, who has blessed us with every spiritual blessing in the heavenly places in Christ," and, "In Him also we have obtained an inheritance" (verses 3, 11).

In Ephesians 2, Paul writes one of the most beautiful and concise passages of Scripture there is, a passage that depicts what life was like before the cross, during the cross and after the cross:

> And you He made alive, who were dead in trespasses and sins, in which you once walked according to the course of this world, according to the prince of the power of the air, the spirit who now works in the sons of disobedience, among whom also we all once conducted ourselves in the lusts of our flesh, fulfilling the desires of the flesh and of the mind, and were by nature children of wrath, just as the others.
>
> But God, who is rich in mercy, because of His great love with which He loved us, even when we were dead in trespasses, made us alive together with Christ (by grace you have been saved), and raised us up together, and made us sit together in the heavenly places in Christ Jesus, that in the ages to come He might *show the exceeding riches of His grace* in His kindness toward us in Christ Jesus. For by grace you

have been saved through faith, and that not of yourselves; it is the gift of God, not of works, lest anyone should boast. *For we are His workmanship, created in Christ Jesus for good works*, which God prepared beforehand that we should walk in them.

Ephesians 2:1–10, emphasis added

In these verses, we begin to see God's intent for grace even more—that He can "show the exceeding riches of his grace" and that "we are his workmanship, created in Christ Jesus for good works." The apostle Paul is hitting on a massive theme that centers on the truth that we are saints of God.

Let's also take a look at Colossians 1:9–12 (emphasis added):

For this reason we also, since the day we heard it, do not cease to pray for you, and to ask that you may be filled with the knowledge of His will in all wisdom and spiritual understanding; *that you may walk worthy of the Lord, fully pleasing Him, being fruitful in every good work and increasing in the knowledge of God*; strengthened with all might, according to His glorious power, for all patience and longsuffering with joy; giving thanks to the Father *who has qualified us to be partakers of the inheritance of the saints in the light.*

As you move away from statements that say you are a sinner and move into living as a righteous person, your attention shifts to being "filled with the knowledge of His will in all wisdom and spiritual understanding" (verse 9). This is what enables you to walk worthy of what God created you for. Make it your prayer and daily pursuit that you would be filled with the knowledge of Him, with divine wisdom and spiritual understanding. Righteous people know what they were and how they became righteous, but they refuse to live under an old identity as "sinners."

We also read in these verses that we can be fruitful in every good work and that we have been qualified to partake of the inheritance God has provided for us as His children. As we gain a new understanding of these things, the conviction of who we are in Christ gets wider and deeper in us, and we find our confidence rising. That is why where deep conviction is, there is also confidence.

Sow Where You Want to Reap

While we often talk about the stewardship of our time, resources and finances, another area of life also requires great attention from us: stewarding the beliefs and convictions we live by and what we wake up every day thinking about. In fact, when you and I recognize what we believe in and the convictions we carry in our hearts, it will determine how we steward our time, resources and finances. If there is no strong sense of what you believe in or what convictions you carry, then you will adopt a lackadaisical approach to life and to stewardship.

To walk in a place of confidence and to know that God trusts you, it is vital that who you think you are lines up with who God thinks you are. Often, who we think we are is not who God thinks we are. It is paramount that believers have an accurate understanding of who they are in Christ. Some believers have an intellectual understanding of it. Some have read about it or have been told about it. But when the rubber meets the road and life is happening, you and I will always live out of what we understand spiritually. Too often, when adversity hits, we have not taken the time beforehand to find out how God truly sees us.

I played baseball for most of my childhood years, all the way up to junior college. When I was ending my junior year in high school, I made a commitment to myself to work hard in the off-season in preparation for my senior year. I set some specific goals and had a workout regimen in mind that would help me with what I wanted to accomplish in my final year of high school.

As my senior year came around and baseball season began, I came into that first week of practice ready to roll. I was conditioned physically, emotionally and mentally for the coming season. Practices normally lasted around two hours, and I usually stayed for an extra thirty minutes or more. I got permission to use the equipment after my coaches and teammates went home. Every day I worked on a different drill. Some days I would swing the bat an extra hundred times or practice stealing bases. I played the position of catcher, and I would do various drills that helped me be quicker and snappier behind the plate.

Often, I would visualize a game scenario where it was the bottom of the last inning with two outs, and I was on first base getting ready to steal second base. I could see the whole game in my head, even though I was the only one on the field. What was I doing? I was sowing where I wanted to reap. I was practicing to the point that when game time came, I did not have to think about what I was going to do. I could simply respond to the game situations with what had now become my natural instincts.

Often in our walk with God, we expect that if we know things intellectually, we are good to go. Knowing things has its place, but if it is all we have, we will soon find out that it may not be enough. When the pressure hits a certain high point and what we know intellectually is not built into our response instincts, whatever situation we are in may overcome us. But you can always tell when you have grasped a full understanding of any area of life, because when a crisis hits, you cannot be moved to change your convictions.

We often talk about changing the culture of our city or nation. Before we can make headway into doing that, we must make sure the culture we envision for our cities and nations is actually taking place inside us and in our lives. We can only give away what we already carry.

In the late 1990s, my parents became pastors of Bethel Church in Redding, California. One of the main things they went after was to promote the understanding that *God is good, and He desires to heal everyone.* This was quite a stance considering that anyone whose belief system was that God brought sickness and disease was easily offended and strongly disagreed. Yet over time, we saw something take place in our church body. Initially, people began to believe intellectually that God is good and desires to heal. Then our belief began to go beyond intellectual assent, and we began to work the reality of it out in our hearts and lives as a body of believers.

When a situation arose where one of our people faced a serious or intimidating disease or sickness, it would reveal the people who truly believed God wants to heal, and it would also reveal the people who were still working toward believing that God desires to heal everyone. Situations like this usually work two ways. They either strengthen people's resolve, or they weaken it. At Bethel, we work to strengthen it. We cultivate room within our culture for people to process through such situations as they journey toward a place of belief.

We made a decision at Bethel to sow where we wanted to reap, and to practice things that would strengthen our resolve in the area of healing. When you do this, you are creating what is called "natural instinct." We work hard as a church body toward confidently being able to speak out and live out the conviction that God desires to heal everyone who is sick. Because we have been sowing in this way consistently, now whenever a crisis or tragedy comes up in our church or area, our natural instinct is to respond with the conviction that God is good and wants to heal everyone. It is nearly impossible to convince any of us otherwise!

Whether it is practicing for a baseball game or practicing to face spiritual challenges like sickness and disease, the principle of sowing where you want to reap is the same. You can sow ahead of time so that later you can reap the kind of instinctual response you will need to see you through in the moment. You will not need to process what to do in a crisis; it will come naturally. Your convictions will bring the confidence to act, because you have been sowing into them ahead of time. In order for your convictions to grow to the point where they give birth to that kind of confidence, you have to manage, invest in and cultivate them.

Friends and Influences

Another aspect of increasing your confidence comes from deciding whom you will let influence you. You will either find yourself influencing others or being influenced by others. Let's look briefly at the importance of whom you surround yourself with and whom you let influence you. The example we will use comes from the moment when the twelve spies were returning to Moses and the people after spying out the Promised Land for forty days:

> Now they departed and came back to Moses and Aaron and all the congregation of the children of Israel in the Wilderness of Paran, at Kadesh; they brought back word to them and to all the congregation, and showed them the fruit of the land. Then they told him, and said: "We went to the land where you sent us. It truly flows with milk and honey, and this is its fruit. Nevertheless the people who dwell in the land are

strong; the cities are fortified and very large; moreover we saw the descendants of Anak there."

Numbers 13:26–28

This is at the point in Israel's journey when they have just experienced being set free from the bondage of Egyptian slavery and now are standing at the doorway to the Promised Land. Moses sends in twelve spies to investigate what they are about to step into. The spies bring back two things: fruit and a report. The report is that there already are people inhabiting the land, and that they are the descendants of Anak and are giants. As the nation hears the bad report, they are confronted with the issue of carrying God's promise that this land is theirs, yet seeing that other people are living there.

Two of the spies, Joshua and Caleb, begin to remind the nation about God's promise. Ten of the spies, however, sway the entire nation from their destiny by saying, in essence, "It is too much. We can't overcome the obstacles." As a result, the nation of Israel wandered in the wilderness for forty years, which became a really long camping trip.

By the time we get to the book of Joshua, we see the nation getting a second chance to go into the Promised Land. We also find out that the ten spies who swayed the nation with their bad report are no longer alive. This extreme example of who influences whom reveals that the people who are able to conquer the impossible are the ones who partner with the promises of God. Joshua leads a nation that is wholly committed to seeing the fulfillment of the promise.

We are responsible for whom we let influence us and whom we surround ourselves with. It is important that we understand the value of this concept because those who influence us in the deep places of our hearts and minds actually shape how we live life. You are a lot like whomever you hang around.

We are a people of promise, and it is vital to surround ourselves with friends and influencers who have God's promises in mind as they live life with us. As believers, we carry great responsibility when it comes to our convictions and the promises of God. Often we will notice that the convictions we carry are also promises from God. As believers, we all have experienced both fulfilled promises and ones yet to be fulfilled. As the nation of Israel followed Joshua into the Promised Land, they all bought into the promise and expected to see its fulfillment. This became a major contributing factor to their success in the coming years.

When my daughters were very young, around two and four, a day came when our oldest daughter was having a rough time and was not in a very obedient state of mind. This went on for a while, and my wife got to the point where she told her, "If you don't stop, you're going to get a spanking."

After Candace said this, our youngest walked up next to her older sister, who was being corrected, and said, "Don't worry. I'll protect you."

Looking back at this instance, it seems cute and funny, but in the moment, it was not quite that. What we see here, though, is a great display of friendship. It is important that you have friends in life who will watch your back and lend their strength to you, even if you are not making great decisions.

In your journey through life as a believer, you will encounter God's promises becoming strong convictions in you, to the point where you will find yourself willing to pay any price or die any death to see them take place. This type of conviction creates a faith in you to do the impossible. These convictions are birthed out of the promises of God, which often causes a deep confidence to rise from within you. True conviction eventually translates into courage, boldness and a relentless pursuit to see the Kingdom come and advance.

If you are lacking confidence, then you may want to evaluate the level of conviction you have in your heart. It has to go beyond an intellectual understanding. If your conviction never goes deeper than the intellect, it may provide you with great teaching or motivational speeches, but ultimately it will yield nothing in terms of you acting on your convictions.

When you have true conviction, however, it begins to affect every cell and fiber of your being. It consumes you. You wake up every day with a sense that "something has to be done," and you have the confidence to do it.

6

---+---

Does God Trust You?

My wife and I are in a season as parents when our girls are in their teen years. The level of trust we all have with each other is expanding and adjusting, which is normal in any relationship. In this progression of trust, there was never a time when we assumed we could not trust our daughters. Our developing trust did not start from a place of "I don't trust you" and go to a place of "Okay, now I trust you." We have always parented from the premise that we trust them. They were not born with an F, a flunking grade, in this area. They were born with an A.

It is important that we do not think our relationship with God started from the premise of His distrusting us. It is important that we do not think it is our responsibility to spend the rest of our life earning God's trust. If God did not trust us, then I assure you, there are a lot of things we would not be doing.

Look back at the ground we have already covered in this book. I hope it suggests to you that God trusts you. He trusts you more than you trust yourself. This thought has the potential to transform a myriad of mindsets and belief systems. It can transform a person's existing relationship with God. It can change a person's view of Him.

Anytime I teach on this subject of trust, it seems to provoke people because it challenges a commonly accepted perception of God—that He does not or cannot trust us. Certain "revelations" and faulty principles like this have become so ingrained in the way the Church and society operate that they can seem to make truly being a son or daughter of the King nearly impossible.

A continual theme of the goodness of God flows throughout Scripture, and it comes to a head in the life of Jesus. We find it in the Lord's Prayer in Matthew 6:10: "Your kingdom come. Your will be done on earth as it is in heaven." When we look at the life of Jesus, He is healing the sick, raising the dead, cleansing the lepers and doing many signs and wonders, as well as letting people know the "good news," which is really good news for us. Jesus is seen inviting people to partake of it, as well as help carry this Kingdom to the world. As we read verse after verse, story after story, we see that interwoven into them is God's heart for humanity and His invitation that we play an active part in seeing His Kingdom come and take place in the world around us.

The apostle Paul tells us multiple times that he is a bondservant of Christ (see Romans 1:1; Galatians 1:10; Titus 1:1). We can look at the life of Moses and see his relationship with God, who spoke to Moses "as one speaks to a friend" (Exodus 33:11 NIV). We read of certain conversations between God and Moses that lead us to conclude that God trusted Moses, and Moses trusted God. At one point, Moses gave God some feedback and God actually listened and deferred to Moses. Wow!

There is no question that God is God, but at the same time, we can have a co-laboring relationship with God. Psalm 25:14 (ESV) reads, "The friendship of the LORD is for those who fear him, and he makes known to them his covenant."

Business Partners

A number of years ago, my family and I were on a ministry trip to a church pastored by a close friend of ours. As the service started and the worship team began to lead us into a time of worship, I noticed an unusual thing was taking place. The worship leader was going into a fresh realm of worship, yet the congregation was not following. As I looked around, I saw people completely disengage from what was opening up in the room through worship. It was odd for me, as my experience has been that the congregation usually follows the worship leader into genuine worship, especially when something is opening up.

As this was happening, my youngest daughter, who was five at the time, began to dance in the front. She did this for a few minutes before it became apparent that she did not feel completely free to dance. Soon she came and stood between Candace and me.

It was obvious that something needed to shift in the atmosphere, so I bent over and spoke into my daughter's ear, "Selah, you've just got to go for it."

She took a deep breath, looked at me with her little determined eyes and then took off dancing throughout the whole room. You could feel the atmosphere shift as she was dancing.

When this took place, I heard the Lord say, "I'm looking for business partners."

There are times when it is clearly God who is doing things, and there are other times when He is looking for those who will partner with Him to see that the things that need to take place happen. In any situation, the devil is vying to see his plan happen, so it is our job to find out what God wants to do in the situation and to respond accordingly.

I think that as long as the ideas and plans are coming from God, most believers do not necessarily have a hard time with the concept that God wants to co-labor with us. It is a common struggle in the hearts and minds of believers, though, to accept that God also wants to co-labor with our ideas. If you stand by the kind of belief system that discounts your ideas and God's willingness to partner with you in them, it diminishes your role as a son or daughter of the King. Under that system, co-laboring with Him will remain one-sided and unfulfilled.

What would you say if my daughters lived a life that was aimed only at doing what I wanted, and their whole purpose in life was to serve me? We all know that as my daughters mature, they will begin to cultivate strong, deep desires of their own. This is a normal, healthy progression of growth. In fact, it happens in our spiritual growth and our relationship with our heavenly Father, too. But somehow the Body of Christ has taken what was supposed to be a beautiful relationship with God, experiencing Him as a good Dad, and morphed it into a dictatorship with an autocratic Father over us who controls our every move.

God has no need to control you or me. The need and desire to control someone comes from fear. God has no fear that makes it necessary for Him to control us. If we think He wants to control our every move so that we do not mess everything up, then we are perceiving Him as fearful of us—a very mistaken perception. Fear is not the currency of heaven, and it is definitely not the tie that binds us to Him. Trust is the tie.

Co-laboring with God

Let's take a look at a couple stories from Scripture about
two men, Joshua and Jehoshaphat, who were co-laborers
with God. Here is the story of Joshua and Jericho that we
find in Joshua 6:1–5:

> Now Jericho was securely shut up because of the children
> of Israel; none went out, and none came in. And the LORD
> said to Joshua: "See! I have given Jericho into your hand, its
> king, and the mighty men of valor. You shall march around
> the city, all you men of war; you shall go all around the city
> once. This you shall do six days. And seven priests shall
> bear seven trumpets of rams' horns before the ark. But the
> seventh day you shall march around the city seven times, and
> the priests shall blow the trumpets. It shall come to pass,
> when they make a long blast with the ram's horn, and when
> you hear the sound of the trumpet, that all the people shall
> shout with a great shout; then the wall of the city will fall
> down flat. And the people shall go up every man straight
> before him."

We find in these verses detailed instructions that God gives
Joshua about what the Israelites are to do when they enter
Jericho. Now look at Joshua 6:10:

> Now Joshua had commanded the people, saying, "You shall
> not shout or make any noise with your voice, nor shall a
> word proceed out of your mouth, until the day I say to you,
> 'Shout!' Then you shall shout."

In this verse, we find Joshua giving instructions, as well.
His instructions are simple: The people are not to talk or
open their mouths until they are told to do so. Personally, I
think he added this because the last time they opened their

mouths, they ended up going back into the wilderness for forty years (see Numbers 13–14). But the key thing I want us to see here is that God and Joshua are co-laboring to accomplish something. The instructions Joshua gives are not part of God's instructions; they are Joshua's.

We need to be aware of the measure of freedom we have when it comes to co-laboring with God, as Joshua was. Another way to look at it is that God likes your ideas, too. He will add His strength to them to make them work.

My youngest daughter has always come up with ideas for creating different things. Her ideas might involve a business she wants to start, her upcoming birthday party or a costume she wants to make for the next big occasion. Over the years, I have watched her interact with my wife in these moments, which often transpire when Selah comes up with a cool, crazy costume idea. Making the costume usually involves some skills she does not possess, so she will go to Candace and say, "Mom, I have this idea for a costume, and this is what it can look like . . ."

My wife, knowing that she is being silently commissioned to accomplish this, obliges Selah by listening to her creative ideas and helping her carry them out successfully. The two of them sit amongst the sewing machine, hot glue gun and fabrics of all colors and textures as my wife works to fulfill the "costume" dream Selah has envisioned. Sometimes it takes a little bit more effort than expected, yet nonetheless, many late nights later Selah will show up wearing her "idea" proudly at some special occasion.

My wife has never regretted helping Selah carry out her ideas. Candace is helping to create a paradigm in Selah's belief system that tells her that whatever idea is stirring up inside her can be accomplished. If she does not possess the skills to do it, then she knows help is available.

When you submit your entire self to God, you are influenced by His nature and His ways. As you come under His influence, the freedom that comes with being a son or daughter of the King will manifest. One of the ways it manifests is in your determination and confidence to carry out the ideas that are stirring inside you. God's eagerness to involve Himself in your affairs is something that becomes obvious when you are in a relationship with Him that is driven not by fear, but by love.

Let's look at a situation similar to Joshua's. In this story, King Jehoshaphat receives a report that three armies are on their way to kill the Israelites. He goes on a fast for three days, crying out to God for help. We read in 2 Chronicles 20:15–17,

> And he [Jahaziel] said, "Listen, all you of Judah and you inhabitants of Jerusalem, and you, King Jehoshaphat! Thus says the LORD to you: 'Do not be afraid nor dismayed because of this great multitude, for the battle is not yours, but God's. Tomorrow go down against them. They will surely come up by the Ascent of Ziz, and you will find them at the end of the brook before the Wilderness of Jeruel. You will not need to fight in this battle. Position yourselves, stand still and see the salvation of the LORD, who is with you, O Judah and Jerusalem!' Do not fear or be dismayed; tomorrow go out against them, for the LORD is with you."

King Jehoshaphat hears the great news that God is going to take care of this battle for them, and they are to stand and watch. Look what happens next:

> So they rose early in the morning and went out into the Wilderness of Tekoa; and as they went out, Jehoshaphat stood and said, "Hear me, O Judah and you inhabitants of Jerusalem: Believe in the LORD your God, and you shall be established; believe His prophets, and you shall prosper." And when he had consulted with the people, he appointed

those who should sing to the LORD, and who should praise the beauty of holiness, as they went out before the army and were saying:

"Praise the LORD,
For His mercy endures forever."

Now when they began to sing and to praise, the LORD set ambushes against the people of Ammon, Moab, and Mount Seir, who had come against Judah; and they were defeated.

Verses 20–22

After hearing from God, King Jehoshaphat instructs his people to put the worship teams in front of the army on the way to the battlefield. This was not part of the instructions God gave in verses 15–17. I would like to propose that King Jehoshaphat put the worship teams out in front of the battle march because they were acting according to their identity, Judah, which means "to be praised and celebrated." In their time of despair, they walked out their identity by lifting up praise to God, the Holy One. When God said to stand and watch, they acted out of who they were and co-labored with God in this situation.

It is fun to see how God allows the ideas of His people to become part of His plan. One of the keys in this story is the importance of living from who you are in your identity. Each believer is a unique being with an identity in Christ. God is so vast and diverse that when He created humanity, He did not duplicate anyone. With that in mind, the value you have in knowing who you are in Christ and who you were created to be is of utmost importance; it will help you navigate the course of life.

It is like the story of the young shepherd boy, David, as he was getting ready to face Goliath. Saul outfitted David with his own armor and weapons in hopes of helping David have a fighting chance with Goliath. David knew this was a bad plan. He was not at all familiar with Saul's gear, and beyond that, it simply was not who he was. David knew what he was capable of, if he stayed true to who he was. By choosing to use his own sling instead of someone else's equipment, he was victorious in slaying the giant.

In the stories of Joshua and Jehoshaphat, we see how God and man partnered together to see battles won and nations advance. The Body of Christ today has to begin to grasp this idea of co-laboring with God in a much greater measure than before. I have a deep conviction that God is waiting for His people to arise and walk in the ideas that burn in their hearts.

A Challenging Notion

One of the most fundamentally challenging things to instill in the hearts and minds of believers is the reality that God trusts them more than they trust themselves. If you grow up in an environment driven by the idea that "we are worth nothing" or "we are horrible people," then the notion that God trusts us becomes extremely challenging, and in some cases, impossible to grasp and live out. In order for us to truly become sons and daughters of the King, there has to be a fundamental shift in how we believe God sees us.

Why would God put Christ in you if He did not trust you? Christ died for us because we cost something; we are of value to Him. If Jesus paid a price so we could be made whole, then it is important to remember that it was a "price" because we have value. You cannot pay a price for something if it does not have value. When I go to a store to buy clothes and I look at the price tag and decide to pay the price on it, I am agreeing that the clothes have value and that I am willing to pay that price. In the same way, when Jesus was headed to the cross, He agreed that the price He was paying was equivalent to the value of what He was dying for.

It is vital that we know that God counts people as highly valuable and delights in them. These verses confirm it for us:

> Then God saw everything that He had made, and indeed it was very good. So the evening and the morning were the sixth day.
>
> Genesis 1:31

> As for the saints who are on the earth, "They are the excellent ones, in whom is all my delight."
>
> Psalm 16:3

> Rejoicing in His inhabited world, and my [wisdom's] delight was with the sons of men.
>
> Proverbs 8:31

It is God's pleasure for the saints to possess the Kingdom:

> But the saints of the Most High shall receive the kingdom, and possess the kingdom forever, even forever and ever. . . . The Ancient of Days came, and a judgment was made in favor of the saints of the Most High, and the time came for the saints to possess the kingdom.
>
> Daniel 7:18, 22

> Do not fear, little flock, for it is your Father's good pleasure to give you the kingdom.
>
> Luke 12:32

Seeing how God sees me invigorates my soul deeply, and my sense of what it means to be a son in His house increases.

I become aware that He is raising me up to be a son of intimacy and authority. As I grow into this place of relationship with Him, I enter a new dimension of trust. This level of trust can feel scary and uncomfortable. It can feel as if I am being pushed to fly before I think I am ready to take flight. But I would rather trust God's push than trust my need to stay in one place.

In any strong, healthy relationship, you will find that trust goes both ways. It is the kind of trust that is rooted in the thought, *I know you will keep me in mind as you make decisions in life.* As a husband, one of the ways I place value on my relationship with my wife is that I make decisions with her in mind. My awareness of Candace's desires and needs stays present and current in my heart as I navigate the daily decisions that are before me. This is the same way I am as a father to my children. My connection to them is evident in how I spend my time and how I give them my attention.

Two Sides of the Same Coin

Back in chapter 2, we covered this book title's phrase "Christ in you," which comes from Colossians 1:27. What we went over in those early pages is one side of the coin. The other side of the same coin can be found later, in Colossians 3:3: "For you died, and your life is hidden with Christ." This theme of being hidden in Christ is similar to a theme found in John 15:4–7:

> Abide in Me, and I in you. As the branch cannot bear fruit of itself, unless it abides in the vine, neither can you, unless you abide in Me.
> I am the vine, you are the branches. He who abides in Me, and I in him, bears much fruit; for without Me you can do

nothing. If anyone does not abide in Me, he is cast out as a branch and is withered; and they gather them and throw them into the fire, and they are burned. If you abide in Me, and My words abide in you, you will ask what you desire, and it shall be done for you.

Abiding in Him and being hidden in Christ are both imperative for every believer. It can be easy when you experience a level of freedom and trust to stray away from the very means of walking in freedom. It would be easy for someone who is not deeply rooted in the death and resurrection of Jesus Christ to become arrogant if all he or she grasped was "Christ in you." It is true that we are charged with the responsibility of walking in great confidence because Christ is in us, but we must also realize that it is essential to abide in Him and stay hidden in Christ. We must remember that we are hidden in Christ, and without Him we can do nothing. These two truths must be kept alive in our hearts and minds all the time. They are not seasonal themes; they are a lifestyle.

A friend of mine called me up one day and asked if I needed some firewood for heating my house in the winter. My reply was yes. We arranged a day to go out and cut firewood deep in the forest. This friend had access to land that was not open to the public, so that next Saturday we headed out of town and began our journey on miles and miles of dirt roads that led us deep into the mountains of Trinity County.

As we made our way down a deep ravine, we came around a corner and my friend pointed at two trees on the ground. They had fallen in a storm the previous year. Even as they lay on the ground, they looked healthy. They had not fallen because of any obvious issues such as disease or rot. My friend told me the reason they had fallen was because this was an area where a logging company had done some "thinning."

When a logging company does thinning, they harvest select trees, but leave alone certain other trees for future harvest. Sometimes what happens as a result is that when the next storm comes through, the trees that are still standing after the thinning will experience wind, rain or snow in a measure they have not experienced before. Back when they were in close proximity to other trees, the density of the forest had protected them. Their roots did not need to go deep because they were shielded by the closeness of the other trees. But once they were unshielded, they were more liable to fall over in adverse weather since their roots did not go down deep enough.

This is a great reminder for us never to stop abiding in Christ and always to make sure our roots are going deeper. If we just worry about going deep, He will take care of the rest.

It's Your Decision. . . .

When you live in covenant and have set your face toward God, you experience the liberty and freedom that can only be found in Christ (see 2 Corinthians 3:16–18). One of the ways trust shows itself in this type of relationship is when it comes to making decisions. In 1999, Candace and I were assistant youth pastors to Banning and Seajay Liebscher at Bethel. It was a great position that we liked, but God was ready for us to take the next step in our ministry. That summer, we were presented with three great opportunities, all within a short period of time. It was a season of open doors for us. We had three invitations, one of which was to help plant a church in Barcelona, Spain. Another was to become part of a thriving, growing ministry in Northern Mexico that cared for thousands of people in various ways. A third was to move to Weaverville, California, as youth pastors.

So began the journey of praying and asking God what we should do. We asked our close family and friends for their thoughts and asked them to pray with us as we searched the heart of God about our next step. As the days went on, we noticed that God was not saying anything; it was as if He had gone into silent mode. It is quite an experience when you are making a major life decision and God is silent. We pressed in harder and got more specific in our prayers.

At some point in the process, Candace and I felt as though God said, "I will honor whatever you decide to do."

Honestly, at first I was not sure if that was God. I was used to having Him tell me what to do and then doing it. Simple obedience—I was more comfortable with that. When it comes to obeying God, it is very easy for me; it is not something I go back and forth on. This time, God was not telling me what to do; He was letting me know that I had the freedom to make a decision and that He would honor it.

This was a major turning point in my relationship with God. I understood that our relationship had deepened in covenant, and I knew more about what it meant to be a son in His house. But it was scary to realize that He trusted Candace and me to make a good decision. Little did we realize that since our faces were turned toward Him, He trusted that we would make this decision with Him in mind. That is what happens in a covenant relationship—it can feel as though "the light is green until it turns red."

The part that makes this kind of scenario scary is the thought, *What if I make the wrong decision?* But we need to remember that this whole process takes place in the context of being in covenant relationship. When you are in covenant relationship with God, you are under His covering and protection, and He is setting you up for success.

When my children do something wrong, my response is not to look at them and say, "I'm done with you; my presence will depart from you." That's silly. Actually, their mistakes initiate fellowship and intimacy between us. I draw near to them and bring correction and discipline aimed at their growing through this moment. Why? Because they are my children, and my ultimate desire above all is to see them become successful people in every way possible. When I interact with them when they have done something wrong, I do things with that goal in mind, not with punishment in mind.

Candace and I considered our three open doors and decided to move to Weaverville to become the youth pastors at Mountain Chapel. To be honest, Weaverville was not at the top of my list when it came to where to go next. I had already lived there from the ages of two to eighteen. We decided, however, to return there. Going back turned out to be one of the wisest decisions we have ever made. What took place in us during those six years in Weaverville was evidence that God honored our decision the way He had said He would.

Silent Mode

Have you noticed that God sometimes seems silent when you are in the middle of making a major decision? One reason could be that He is in some way letting you know that because you are in covenant with Him and you have set your face toward Him, He will honor whatever decision you make.

If God makes all the decisions for us, then we will have nothing to give an account for at the end of our lives. It is tough to be accountable for something about which you had no choice or freedom. We all know a day is coming when we will stand before Him and give an account of our lives.

There is a responsibility involved for us when He puts us on this earth. His desire is not that we be controlled by Him, but that we should be empowered by Him.

So far, we have been building off the foundation that Christ lives in you and that His light shines from you. We have also learned that we are going in one direction—from glory to glory—because we have set our faces toward Him. As we find ourselves in this position, it reinforces that we are more than just His slaves and servants; we are also His friends.

John 15:15 reads, "No longer do I call you servants, for a servant does not know what his master is doing; but I have called you friends, for all things that I heard from My Father I have made known to you." Romans 6:22 reads, "But now having been set free from sin, and having become *slaves of God*, you have your fruit to holiness, and the end, everlasting life" (emphasis added).

These are some of the passages of Scripture that touch on the three words *slaves*, *servants* and *friends*. As we read through Scripture, we see numerous examples of people who walked in friendship with God, but we also see the fact that they were His slaves and/or servants. A true friend is willing to become a slave for another friend, and a true friend will become a servant in a heartbeat. Being a friend of God means you are willing to offer yourself as a slave and a servant. I know that when you begin to live this out, you will begin to realize that the trust between you and God goes both ways. God really does trust you more than you realize.

7

——— + ———

Permission to Be Great

The price of greatness is responsibility.
—Winston Churchill

One of my priorities in life is to understand and demonstrate the Kingdom. I deeply desire to know the things of God and to make them known. In order to know the things of God and grasp some of the ways in which He works, we can start in Genesis and look at how He created the heavens and the earth, and for what purpose. Capturing an idea of what was in God's heart at the conception and birth of Creation gives us a glimpse into His nature.

Reading through the Bible and history books, we can follow humanity's start in the Garden and see our progression from there. It has been a wild journey through the centuries. First we see the effects of the Fall of man, then we see the answer in the cross and resurrection of Jesus Christ. The human race has had some incredible accomplishments and some extreme failures, but nonetheless, we have continually moved forward. One of the reasons for this can be found in Genesis 1, the chapter that records Creation itself.

> Then God said, "Let Us make man in Our image, according to Our likeness; let them have dominion over the fish of the sea, over the birds of the air, and over the cattle, over all the earth and over every creeping thing that creeps on the earth." So God created man in His own image; in the image of God He created him; male and female He created them. Then God blessed them, and God said to them, "Be fruitful and multiply; fill the earth and subdue it; have dominion over the fish of the sea, over the birds of the air, and over every living thing that moves on the earth."
>
> And God said, "See, I have given you every herb that yields seed which is on the face of all the earth, and every tree whose fruit yields seed; to you it shall be for food. Also, to every beast of the earth, to every bird of the air, and to everything that creeps on the earth, in which there is life, I have given every green herb for food"; and it was so.
>
> Genesis 1:26–30

God decided to make man and commanded, "Let Us make man in Our image" (verse 26). It was in this moment that the journey of humanity began.

Arrogance or Confidence?

We have already covered a bit of ground in regard to recognizing that we can do nothing without Christ since we are hidden in Him, and that it is equally important to remember that He abides in us. Many of us are familiar with Philippians 4:13, "I can do all things through Christ who strengthens me," a verse we commonly quote in challenging situations. This powerful verse clearly defines who it is who brings us strength. We are a new creation because of Christ living in us, so we are able to live in a place of great strength, resolve and confidence. Living our lives with an awareness of Christ abiding in us brings us strength and creates confidence and faith in what is possible. When you look at the great men and women of the faith, they seemed to approach life differently than most. They had a great sense of trust in what is actually possible because they knew God was on their side. To some, they seemed like the crazy ones who did not think things through. History tells a different story. They were the ones who believed in the impossible taking place and who carried a pure confidence that allowed them to accomplish what was in front of them. Why? They simply were aware of who their Daddy was.

This is the intended norm for every believer—to live with a pure confidence in who God is. I would like to take you a step further into this incredible realm of having a biblical, healthy confidence. Let's start by looking at the difference between confidence and arrogance. As I mentioned at the beginning of chapter 5, *confidence is driven by what it can give, and arrogance is motivated by what it can gain.*

When as a believer, you walk in a confidence apart from the revelation that Christ lives in you and that you abide in Him, your confidence can easily turn into pride and arrogance. Arrogance is carnally focused and will lead you to a place where it is all about you and what you can gain. The proper way to approach confidence, then, without it turning into arrogance, is to realize that Christ abides in you and you in Him. The realization of this truth keeps us living as confident believers, not arrogant ones.

Let's take a look at three different passages that carry a similar theme:

God be merciful to us and bless us, and cause His face to shine upon us. Selah. That Your way may be known on earth, your salvation among all nations.

Psalm 67:1–2

Let your light so shine before men, that they may see your good works and glorify your Father in heaven.

Matthew 5:16

In the ages to come He might show the exceeding riches of His grace in His kindness toward us in Christ Jesus.

Ephesians 2:7

The verses from Psalms and Matthew highlight the theme that when God's face shines on us and we let our light shine, the result or fruit will be that God will get the glory and His salvation will be known in the nations. The Ephesians passage explains what will happen when His grace is extended toward us; it will reveal His riches in the ages to come. Realizing that He is the light and that His grace has been given to us should create in us a confidence that can only be explained by the fact that it is because we are His. It should be the heart of every believer to live and walk in a place of pure confidence.

The definition of *confidence* can include a belief in one's own abilities, a self-assurance, a belief in one's ability to succeed, a trusting relationship, or a relationship based on trust and intimacy.[1] It is important to understand that when

1. *The Free Dictionary* online, s.v. "confidence," http://www.thefreedictionary .com/confidence.

we were created, God gave us gifts, skills and abilities, and how we use them—whether for Him or not—is up to us. Often we see people who are not believers in Jesus Christ accomplishing some amazing things—making great music, inventing things, solving world problems or helping people. That is the result of their being equipped with gifts, skills and abilities. Since you and I are believers, we choose to use our gifts and attributes for God's glory. When we know Christ is in us and we cultivate trust and intimacy with Him, it allows us to believe in the abilities we have at hand and wholeheartedly believe we will succeed. That is not arrogance; that is pure confidence in God and the way He created us.

Looking at the life of Jesus, we see a Man who was a revolutionary, a miracle worker, a teacher and a lover of humanity. One thing we often overlook, though, is His incredible ability to lead people. His ability to lead people, specifically His disciples, challenges me. Incredibly, He led in such a way that when He ascended to be with the Father, the Kingdom exploded on the earth. How many leaders do you know whose ministry increased after they left?

One of the key things I have found is that through His leadership, Jesus instilled in His disciples an incredible sense of ownership and responsibility. This is evident in the way they lived their lives purely dedicated to the cause of the Kingdom, even unto death.

The Road to Greatness

My dream is that when I am done leading something, it will increase after I have moved on. As a leader who has some influence, I like to remind myself of Luke 9:46–48, where Jesus demonstrated His unique style of leadership. His ability to lead a diverse group of men and truly alter the course of history is a testament to His leadership and His understanding of people.

> Then a dispute arose among them as to which of them would be greatest. And Jesus, perceiving the thought of their heart, took a little child and set him by Him, and said to them, "Whoever receives this little child in My name receives Me; and whoever receives Me receives Him who sent Me. For he who is least among you all will be great."
>
> Luke 9:46–48

We find here an interesting little interaction between Jesus and His disciples. The disciples are talking about which one of them is the greatest. This incident takes place in the chain of events Luke records in chapter 9 that we could call a "great ministry trip." At the beginning of Luke 9, the disciples were given power and authority to do signs and wonders. After they went out and came back again, they told Jesus about all that had happened and how the power and authority really worked. Then they saw Jesus multiply food to feed over five thousand people. Then they saw a demonized boy get delivered. By this point, the disciples were beginning to feel pretty good about ministry because they were seeing successes everywhere. Then we come upon the above passage where they begin to argue about who is the greatest.

I am not surprised that this argument took place. When you hang around someone who is pretty good at what he or she does and that person teaches and empowers you, a natural thing takes place in the process—you begin to gain confidence in yourself. When the disciples began to argue about who was the greatest, it was because they were beginning to live out the things that Jesus did every day.

Imagine being in the disciples' shoes and realizing that you were doing the impossible. Imagine seeing all those signs and wonders take place. In Scripture we find two common responses to being with Jesus. Some ended up hating Him, which is what the religious leaders of the day did. Some ended up considering themselves the greatest thing ever to walk the earth, because of their association with Him. That was where the disciples were in this case, when they were caught discussing which one of them was the greatest.

I am amazed at how little understood this story of their argument is. Often, it is taught with applications that are not found in the story. We all have heard it taught that Jesus despises pride and really does not like it when you talk about who is the greatest. As a result, we have developed specific discipleship programs for people who have pride issues. These programs usually take such people right out of ministry and put them in a six-month program to make sure they understand how bad pride is. Then when they complete that, they are put on a two-year probation period to see if pride ever surfaces again. If all goes well and they stay humble, a committee approves them when they are deemed ready to be put back on the front lines.

That is a normal response to pride in the Body of Christ, but what actually takes place in the story is quite different from what it seems. Jesus never even rebukes His disciples for discussing who is the greatest. What He does is absolutely stunning; He uses a child as an example and says that if you become like a child, you will be great.

What is He doing? He is giving His disciples *permission to be great*, and then He gives them instructions on how to be the greatest in a healthy way. His comments show them how to fulfill the desire of their hearts.

Most counselors or others in the Church who make an effort to help people struggling with pride do not spend a lot of time giving them permission to be great. They spend more time letting such people know that they are not allowed to strive for greatness, and that being a believer is more about how incapable or incompetent they are and how much they therefore need God.

Somehow we believers feel that if we tear ourselves down enough, it reveals how truly amazing God is. Why do we think it makes sense to criticize something God has created to make Him look great? Why do we think we need to make ourselves look incompetent before He can work through us? Although Jesus does not condone pride in the story we have been talking about, He does encourage His disciples along in their desire to be great. He just goes about it by redirecting them onto a different path toward greatness. The goal of achieving greatness, however, remains.

What we often misunderstand is that the desire to be great and amazing is normal. I talked at the beginning about how normal and acceptable it is for children to want to be significant, to want to climb higher and go farther and be somebody when they grow up. Inside every child is the sense that he or she is destined for greatness. Of course, there is an unhealthy desire that can arise from that if it goes toward arrogance instead of confidence, but Jesus is not as afraid of that tendency as we are. He knows how to redirect it.

Let me propose to you that we are more afraid of people walking in pride than Jesus is. Am I suggesting that pride is okay? Absolutely not! Yet sometimes when we are scared of something, we do not respond the way we should. Often, we are afraid of things that do not concern Jesus. In His leadership, He just redirected what was unhealthy in His disciples and showed them a better road to follow toward greatness. Sometimes it is really as simple as rerouting what is in our heart.

In this type of conversation, Romans 12:3 is a frequently used verse: "For I say, through the grace given to me, to everyone who is among you, *not to think of himself more highly than he ought to think*, but to think soberly, as God has dealt to each one a measure of faith" (emphasis added). Often people mistake this verse as meaning we ought to think of ourselves as worthless and pointless. I find it rather confusing that the Body of Christ spends a lot of time ridiculing, demeaning and debasing itself. We applaud this as humility, when we are actually spiritualizing a dysfunction. It is unnecessary to criticize ourselves to reveal the power of grace. This verse we just read shows up in the context of Paul writing about a strong theme—our need to realize that we are members of the Body:

> For as we have many members in one body, but all the members do not have the same function, so we, being many, are one body in Christ, and individually members of one another. Having then gifts differing according to the grace that is given to us, let us use them: if prophecy, let us prophesy in proportion to our faith; or ministry, let us use it in our ministering; he who teaches, in teaching; he who exhorts, in exhortation; he who gives, with liberality; he who leads, with diligence; he who shows mercy, with cheerfulness.
>
> Romans 12:4–8

When you read verse 3 in this context, the main emphasis is that if you are one part of the Body but you think you are another part, then you will think and operate outside your role in the Body. That is when you begin to think too "highly" of yourself. This passage is pointing out that we have different gifts, and we need to use our gifts in proportion to the measure of faith we have. Paul is teaching us to live out our gifts according to the grace given and not from the standpoint of putting ourselves down.

In the rest of Romans 12, Paul exhorts us to live from a place of love. Love is the game changer. When you live your life in full confidence and from a foundation of love, you will then spend your days for the benefit of the people around you. This is the confidence you are called to walk in, a confidence driven by what it can give to the world you live in. When this confidence is pulsating in your veins, you wake up every day with a sense of purpose because you have been called by God to see His Kingdom come and His will be done. The reality of Christ in you and you abiding in Him comes to life in ways only possible because of the grace of God working in you. You know you cannot do anything without Him, and you can do everything with Him. Confidence is not the absence of humility.

Steward Your Heart

One of our greatest responsibilities as believers is to steward our hearts. We know there are carnal desires and godly desires inside us; our role is to be aware of what those are and to steward them well or deal with them accordingly.

Numerous times, I have had people come up and ask, "How do you know if you're working too hard for something or you're promoting yourself?"

I usually respond with a question: "Can you tell when you are striving?"

Most people answer yes to that. If you have the ability to recognize when you are striving, let that be an indicator of when you are pushing too much or working too hard for something—or trying to be great. For me, this is a simple way to steward my heart. Each of us needs to be diligent in our passions, calling and desires. However, when striving becomes a driving force in us, then we begin to open the doors for arrogance and pride to come live in us.

I believe that one of the things God is adjusting in the heart of His Church is the way in which we lead. He wants us to learn to lead people the way Jesus led them. Can you imagine a scenario where believers all over the world walk with permission to be great? All the talk we hear of advancing the Kingdom into every part of society would be fulfilled. People would be living out of their hearts and not their heads. It would be rare to find someone doing something he or she does not love doing. Communities around the world would be creating so much momentum that ideas would come forth that would alter the course of history.

One of the things we aim to cultivate in our environment here at Bethel and in our city of Redding is this very thing—a church body whose people know they carry the responsibility for seeing their city touched by God. We take ownership of that. We continue to feed the poor, and we work to help take care of those who are in desperate need of the basics of food, clothing and shelter. Along with that, we aim to affect the economics of our city and region. Many people around us live in a poverty cycle, and we know that we are part of the solution in breaking this cycle.

Our vision for our church family is that its members would be the ones to see people get saved, healed and set free, and that our church family also would start businesses that provide commerce and opportunities for others. We want to see members of our church family doing things like coaching little league baseball (or any other sport) and increasing the quality of life for families who call this city their home. For some, it means getting involved in the city council scene. Instead of complaining to the city fathers and mothers, they come forward and offer genuine solutions to the many issues our city faces in trying to reverse social statistics that lower the quality of life. We at Bethel want to walk out the call of every believer to preach the Gospel, heal the sick and do good on the earth.

There will always be great individuals throughout history, but I dream of a day when an entire generation of people is referred to as "a great generation that believed and conquered the impossible." For this to take place, a shift in our thinking needs to take place. We all need to carry the idea of personal ownership and responsibility. It begins when people embrace the idea that God designed them for greatness, and that He has given them gifts, talents and skills. It is up to each of us to determine what part we play in the grand scheme of things, but first, we need to give ourselves and each other permission to be great!

It Can Get Messy

When you create a place where the permission to be great is given, that does not mean things will not get messy or other issues will not arise. In some ways, things may get really messy. Immediately after Jesus gives His disciples permission to be great, we read in Luke 9:49–50,

> "Master," said John, "we saw someone driving out demons in your name and we tried to stop him, because he is not one of us."
>
> "Do not stop him," Jesus said, "for whoever is not against you is for you."

Jesus had just redirected their desire to be great, and John is pointing out with concern that others who are not a part of their group are doing what they are doing. Jesus simply answers that they are on the same team.

What Jesus is doing is unraveling the disciples' "elitism" paradigm. Elitism can often be found in a person or group of people who think what they are doing is all about themselves. When you and I are going about doing the Lord's work, we need to make sure that our perspective on life and what we do is not about us. It is about God and His people whom we are called to serve. The will of God for our lives is more about Him and the people around us than it is about us. His will is bigger than us, and anytime we think it is all about us, we are veering off course.

The next few verses, Luke 9:51–56, show us another incident:

> Now it came to pass, when the time had come for Him to be received up, that He steadfastly set His face to go to Jerusalem, and sent messengers before His face. And as they went, they entered a village of the Samaritans, to prepare for Him. But they did not receive Him, because His face was set for the journey to Jerusalem. And when His disciples James and John saw this, they said, "Lord, do You want us to command fire to come down from heaven and consume them, just as Elijah did?"
>
> But He turned and rebuked them, and said, "You do not know what manner of spirit you are of. For the Son of Man did not come to destroy men's lives but to save them." And they went to another village.

First they are arguing about who is the greatest, next they are battling elitism, and now they are talking about killing an entire city. You can see this progression from the beginning of Luke 9 to the end. These disciples are feeling pretty powerful. At this point in the story, Jesus does rebuke them. But that necessity does not stop Him from empowering them.

He still empowered them long before most leadership training programs would have deemed them "ready."

I believe Jesus is rewriting here how to raise up world-changers. His model seemed to be, "I'll teach you along the way." This model can be scary and tough to implement for those of us who lead other people. Often we want proof that people are really "ready" to lead before we let them lead. Yet Jesus demonstrated for us that He was not afraid of His followers making mistakes. That did not mean He was okay with all their mistakes or messes; it just meant He did not let their mistakes stop Him from empowering His disciples.

The Power of Covenant

In the three years of Jesus' ministry with His disciples, one vital and often unnoticed ingredient was *covenant*. He and His disciples had a sort of covenant relationship. Throughout the gospels, we see something in the disciples that can only be described as complete surrender and abandonment to the cause of Christ. They put everything on the line for Jesus.

In John 6:56, we find Jesus talking about what is possibly the most offensive teaching in all His ministry when He says, "He who eats My flesh and drinks My blood abides in Me, and I in him."

After He continues to elaborate on this idea, the crowds disperse. Even the disciples struggle with this "cannibalistic" idea Jesus is teaching.

Jesus eventually turns to His disciples and says, "Do you also want to go away?" (verse 67).

Peter immediately responds, "Lord, to whom shall we go? You have the words of eternal life" (verse 68).

Peter's statement reveals the essence of the covenant he had made with Jesus. He had nowhere else to go since he had gotten rid of everything else to follow Him. Sometimes you have to get rid of all your other options in order to commit fully to only one. Peter also recognized where the source of "life" was. Because he recognized this and because he had made a covenant with his life to follow Jesus, he was able to navigate Jesus' "offensive" statement, and in the midst of being offended, he was able to hear the truth.

We often do not realize the power of covenant. Anytime we find Jesus talking directly to the disciples and giving them a command, it is important to remember that He is talking to a group of men who have given their lives to follow Him. They were in covenant, and it was from covenant that they were sent out. It was not from a place of acquaintanceship. The deeper you are in relationship with Jesus or with a group of believers, the more willing you are to explore and learn the ways of the Kingdom. Covenant relationships are one of the essentials to any culture where the Kingdom is the priority. Covenant is the incubator where beautiful things take place.

Covenant does not have to involve some weird or dramatic event in our lives; it can be a simple yet immovable commitment to the Lord Jesus Christ and to each other for the cause of Christ. Covenant is more about whom the covenant is made with than it is about you.

Unfortunately, in our times a lot of "covenants" are made for only as long as it benefits the partners. Marriages take place based on the premise that, "As long as I benefit, I'll honor this commitment." The purity of true covenant, however, is, "I'll do anything to serve you, love you and care for you." When this true covenant takes place on both sides of a relationship, it forms a deeply rooted commitment to each other, with the potential of creating a learning environment along the way.

I believe the reason Jesus did not spend a whole lot of time rebuking His disciples as they were dealing with pride and elitism was that He was living life with them and teaching them along the way. This is essential for us to understand and live out. The dominant context of the disciples' lives is that they were in covenant and in community with Jesus and each other. That is how they were able to grow and do things that changed history. Jesus modeled it for them by leading the way.

We were not meant to become completely isolated from each other. As Proverbs 18:1 says, "A man who isolates himself seeks his own desire; he rages against all wise judgment." My wife and I are pastors at Bethel Church in Redding, and one of our main priorities is to build community and family within a church of our size that has our unique mandate. We have worked diligently to see this take place.

A couple years ago, as we began to lay out our heart and vision in front of the church body, we made this statement: "Our goal is *not only* to build community and family. It is the starting point for every person that calls Bethel home. It is from community and family that you are launched to change the world."

It was important for our church body to know that we are not trying to "end" in community, but rather, we are making community the starting point for the call of God on our lives—to change the world.

When it comes to the Body of Christ, note that if we build community only for the sake of community, in the long run we will make a lot of ponds where the water comes in but does not go out. That is a scary situation; the water gets murky, algae forms and it gets pretty nasty. As the Body of Christ in community together, we need to have a river flowing through us and out of us that brings life wherever it may lead.

Jesus had a strong purpose in mind for His disciples, so the community and covenant they formed ultimately was aimed at fulfilling that one purpose—to make known to the world that the Kingdom had come and that its King, Jesus, is the way, the truth and the life. That is what their community was established in covenant to give the world.

A Unique Opportunity

The Body of Christ has a unique opportunity to help people come into covenant in a community with the same purpose that Jesus established right from the start. The Body must become a place where people can live in pure confidence, with permission to be great. Their confidence will not be the arrogant sort that is attracted by personal gain; it will be the passionate sort that is determined to see what it can give the world through helping the Kingdom come into every aspect of society.

Whether you are a leader, a parent, a boss or are simply leading yourself, here are some questions for you that will help you create an environment in which permission to be great can become a reality:

- Am I comfortable around powerful, driven or strong people? If not, what steps can I take to defuse my discomfort and give these people permission to be great and to do great things for God?
- Do I understand the difference between confidence and arrogance? Am I asking myself, *What can I give?* or *What can I gain?*
- Do I see how Jesus led differently by creating an environment that allowed His disciples to make mistakes and grow in their confidence?

- If I or the people around me become really confident because Christ is in us and we are abiding in Him, what is there ultimately to be afraid of? Do I see how, with that kind of pure confidence in God, we can change the world?

- Do I work on establishing community not just for its own sake, but for the sake of bringing the Kingdom to earth? Have those of us in my community covenanted with our lives to fulfill that purpose?

Depending on how you answer the questions above, you can establish a foundation through your leadership where the people around you have permission to go for it, even if they make some mistakes and messes that they have to clean up along the way. In the learning process, they will become great and do great things for God.

With that goal in mind, take some time to ponder your answers carefully. It will initiate a process in you that will help you identify some things you may need to address in yourself and in your community of believers. Remember, you have a unique opportunity to create a pathway for divine greatness to flourish in you and in the people around you, so that together you can covenant to preach the Gospel, heal the sick and do good on the earth. God trusts you to carry out His purposes more than you trust yourself.

8

———— + ————

The Box

A friend of mine was sitting across the table from me in a local coffee shop, giving me an update on how his life and business were going. It encouraged me to hear that he was experiencing breakthrough in his personal life and also seeing success in the business he is leading. A number of years ago, he left full-time church ministry to move to Redding, California, to become part of the Bethel family. After moving out here, he took a job at a local business, mainly to provide for his family.

As we drank our coffee, he mentioned that in spite of things going really well and in spite of noticing the favor of God on his life and business, he was still holding back "5 percent" of himself. The reason was in case a church position opened up somewhere. If it did, he wanted to be ready to jump on the opportunity. This was the first time in his life that he was working in the marketplace, and he was surprised at how well he was doing. In his heart, though, he wanted to do something else. He said he would rather be working full-time in a church setting. To him, his marketplace job was just keeping him in a holding pattern until something else opened up.

As I listened to my friend talk, I thought to myself that it would be one thing if he were not doing well at his job. That would make his wanting to do something else and his holding back from a full commitment understandable. But he was highly successful in his job and was experiencing a great deal of favor. He was also being promoted very quickly, and he carried real wisdom about how to restructure the West Coast division of this particular business. Even in giving less than 100 percent of himself, his results were stunning.

Thinking about my friend's 5 percent reserve, I asked him a simple question: "Are you afraid of being put in a box?"

His reply was also simple: "Yes, I am!"

My friend felt that he would miss an opportunity to go back into church ministry if he gave himself fully to his current business. He also felt that, in a way, he would become unavailable or go off the radar.

"What is it you are afraid of?" I asked him.

"I don't want to be viewed a certain way and get put into this box as a businessman and not a pastor," he replied. "If I give myself fully to the business, then I won't fulfill the prophetic words on my life."

"So it sounds as if you don't really trust God with your future," I said.

He thought about that for a minute and did not really know what to say. Suddenly he was realizing that he did not trust God with his future the way he should.

Fear of Man

Two things were taking place with my friend. First, he was embracing the fear of man, which led him not to trust God with his future. His trust was in the hands of man to take care of his future.

Second, he thought the prophetic words spoken over him would come to pass in a certain way, but he was being too narrow in his thinking. It is not unusual for us to interpret or understand prophetic words over our lives through a certain lens colored by how we think they will and should happen. I have learned that prophetic words are rarely wrong, but the process of how and when they come to pass and what that looks like in the end often plays out completely differently from what we originally imagine.

Because of my limited understanding, more than once I have had a certain idea in my mind of how a prophetic word would come to pass and what that would look like in my life. Whenever I have approached a prophetic word with that kind of preconceived journey superimposed over it, though, God has had a surprise in store for me. I have realized in the end that the word was being fulfilled while I was unaware of it.

Why did this happen? Because I had the journey and the process all mapped out in my mind, and I was on the lookout for something that matched my mental picture. Meanwhile, however, the fulfillment was unfolding in a different direction. When a prophetic word is given, the destination is inevitable. The journey, however, is a mystery that is about to be revealed.

As my friend and I talked about all this for a bit, it was apparent that the box he was trying so hard to avoid was a direct result of his fear of man. The box is an idea we make up in our minds, but it does not truly exist. It is made out of the lies we believe and out of our fear of certain things.

I have personally experienced how the fear of man can form a box around us that narrows how we think we ought to live our lives and what we think we should do with them. I have seen it happen to other people, too. Any time fear is in your heart, be aware of your thoughts and decisions. Often our faulty paradigms create these boxes, which in the end can limit us or deter us from expressing who God made us to be.

Earlier in this book we addressed the phrases "Christ in you" and having the "light in you" and how those revelations expand our view of what ministry can look like. As believers, it is granted to us to do everything in life as worship unto the King. That makes it vitally important that we address any fear of man within us and break any paradigm that limits our thinking about how we should live our lives as believers. Not confronting these things means we are more afraid of what people think than of what God thinks. That is how we create our own little boxes built by fear.

We all have boxes we have to deal with, but the fear of man does particularly crazy things to us. Whenever we are boxed in by fear, we make decisions that are not exactly great. A normal response to fear in your life is to do whatever you can to control the situation you are in. The need to be in control is a major piece of evidence pointing to the presence of fear. Instead of trusting God, we work tirelessly to control the outcome.

Fear of man usually comes in one of two varieties: "I am scared of you" or "I care more about what you think or say than anything else." I think most people identify with the latter, which is a thinking process that elevates other people's views above God's view in our minds. That will end up steering how we think and live.

Here are a handful of questions that may help you identify whether you are living in a box or laboring under the fear of man:

1. Do you know what God's heart for you is? If the answer is no, then you may find yourself trying to fill the void inside or your need for affection and attention through the people around you.

2. Do you seek people's attention more than God's? After you accomplish something, do you find yourself eliciting a response from the people around you?

3. Do you feel primarily accountable to God for your life and decisions, or do you feel as if you would rather get feedback from the people around you first? Your primary source of attention and affection should be God, and your sense of belonging should come from Him. Once those things are established, you will not feel as if you live or die by other people's attention or opinions.

4. Do you raise your kids, work at your job, teach at a school or do whatever you do as worship and ministry to the King? If you feel trapped or do not feel free to express who you are to the core in these places, it is possible that you have a faulty paradigm in place that is limiting you.

Living in a box or under the fear of man is an inferior way to live. To walk in the true confidence God destined you to have, it is paramount that you learn to break free from the fear of man. As long as you entertain that fear, it will keep you trapped in its imaginary box. Finding your freedom is not something you can approach flippantly. It takes real diligence—and in some cases violence—to break free.

Journeying toward Freedom

Let's go over five principles or steps that can help a person break free from the fear of man. This is not an exhaustive list by any means, but it is a great place for someone to start in the journey toward becoming free.

1. Perfect love casts out fear.
2. Truth alone can expose the lies.

3. Build the wall that is in front of you.

4. God is a good teacher.

5. Self-promotion is the absence of trust in God.

Perfect Love Casts Out Fear

The remedy for all fear is wrapped up in the word *love*. First John 4:18 reads, "There is no fear in love; but perfect love casts out fear, because fear involves torment. But he who fears has not been made perfect in love."

For a very long time, love has been one of the most sung about and most talked about topics in our society. Humanity has a natural longing to love and be loved. It is in the fabric of who we are as people. Unfortunately, the word *love* has been relegated to a lustful idea that has become perverted and twisted. That kind of "love" has left billions empty-hearted. Real love is deeper than sex.

My wife and I have had the privilege of pastoring many people over the years. One of the common things we have found in helping people is that the ones who are missing love in their lives are usually the ones who have issues. When they do not know that they are loved by God and by other people, they typically struggle with fear. Each person shows it differently. Some find themselves in a perpetual cycle of anger toward life and its situations. Some settle for second best in life. Others find themselves hoping a relationship will cure the void of love inside them. Still others turn to substance abuse and create a lifestyle of addictions. The effects are different on every person, but the reason is usually the same—in the absence of love, they have embraced fear. When you embrace fear, the worst "you" comes to the surface.

The only way to cast out fear is by letting love in. The source of all love is God Himself. Not only does God know how to love; He *is* love. He is the very definition and expression of love.

You cannot experience love unless you are willing to let go of fear. This is not a negotiating process where a discussion takes place about who lets go first. Often this process of letting go is necessary so you can face your fears. If fear is in your life, you must be diligent and be willing to let go of it. If living in fear is all you know and it is your comfort zone, then yes, it can be challenging to let it go. But remember that it is inferior to what you desire the most—love. Fear and love cannot live together.

It is tough to love and be loved if you are not humble and vulnerable. Some common fears when it comes to being humble and making yourself vulnerable with someone may include these:

- You may be afraid that you will appear weak or frail in the other person's eyes.
- You may fear that the person whom you are opening up to will not protect you.
- You may think that the person will come to an inaccurate conclusion about your character.
- You may wonder if the person will tell others about you.
- You may wonder if you can really trust that the person will cover you and look out for you.

When you are in a relationship, friendship or community of people that truly operates out of love, though, you will experience a high level of liberty. Perfect love casts out fear, and genuine love creates an environment that allows you to be "you." Then you are able to give away love because you have received it.

Truth Alone Can Expose the Lies

The second principle or step I want to mention in breaking off the fear of man is acknowledging what is truth. When the truth is seen, it exposes all lies. Whenever you know the truth, you can recognize lies and counterfeits. We tend to think if we just work really hard to get rid of all the "bad" things in our lives, everything will work out. But what we focus on is usually what we will become. Whatever is alive in our lives is alive because we are feeding it.

My dad, Bill Johnson, shares an illustration about people whose occupation it is to find counterfeit currency. When they are training to become experts at identifying counterfeit currency, they do not study the counterfeits; they study real currency. Once they become intimately familiar with the real thing, it becomes easier to recognize the counterfeits. In the same way, as we become familiar with the truth of God, we are able to identify the lies of the enemy.

It is important that every believer be able to identify the real thing when it comes to the promises of God and what He says about His children. We are each responsible to steward these things in our lives. Any time I come across people who are struggling with who they are and what they are doing in life, I immediately help them remember or find out what the promises of God are and what God says about them. If a person stewards God's words and promises well, he or she will no longer be steered by the fear of man or by insecurities.

My process for stewarding the promises of God and what He says about me is to keep a record of them in written form, and if possible, in audio form. I have documents and audio files on my iPad and laptop of the various prophetic words and promises God has spoken to me or had other people speak over me through the years. They serve as my compass and one of the ways of strengthening myself in the Lord. Whenever the fear of man is working to find a place in my heart, I read and/or listen to what God says about me. One of the highest priorities in my life is to be led by what God says about me above anything else.

Confronting the fear of man in ourselves and breaking free of it can be an exhausting process. But remember that the diligence you put toward this process is building strength in you. You gain strength by encountering resistance. This is true in the natural, mental and spiritual. When you go to the gym and lift weights, you are submitting your body to resistance. When you encounter resistance, you counter it back with your strength. When your muscles do this over and over, it builds muscle strength and you are able to handle even more resistance.

If you find yourself in a deep pattern of the fear of man, then it will require persistence on your part to build the strength to resist it. Often you will not "feel" the promises of God; you will have to choose to side with the truth and with His promises. Eventually, your choice will translate from something you choose to believe into something that every fiber of your being experiences.

Build the Wall That Is in Front of You

The third step to breaking free from the fear of man involves giving attention to what is going on in your life at the moment. Look at the example of Nehemiah, a man who served in the courts of King Artaxerxes (see Nehemiah 1–3). On one particular day, Nehemiah has a sad countenance as he is serving wine to the king. The king asks why he is sad, and Nehemiah shares how his city lies in ruins and he longs to do something about it. At Nehemiah's request, the king sends him to help rebuild the city of his fathers.

We can only imagine the upheaval, stress and distractions the people who went back to rebuild that city were going through. The morale of the people was low as they stood in the midst of a ruined city and society. As this story unfolds, one of the defining moments comes when Nehemiah gives them a very simple task of building the wall that is in front of them. They were to make repairs to the wall around the city "each in front of his own house" (Nehemiah 3:28). I believe that when it comes to setting priorities in life, this is one of the most profound instructions in the Bible.

Sometimes in life's most chaotic moments, the answer lies in the simplicity of it all. This instruction to build the wall that was in front of them was simple, yet it was key to seeing the city rebuilt and reestablished. Sometimes when we look at the grand scope of things, it is easy to get distracted by how much needs to be done, and it is also easy to desire to get involved in something that is not in front of you and to go somewhere else. Yet something powerful happens when we decide simply to do what is in front of us.

Commonly, what is right in front of us is the last thing we want to do or want give our time to. There is always greener grass somewhere else or something that seems way more appealing. One of the greatest privileges in life, though, is to convert a field of weeds into one that is full of green grass. The mandate of every believer is to step into a dire situation and see it turn around.

I would like to challenge you to approach life differently by focusing on "the wall that is in front of you." The wall that is in front of you is made up of the things in your life that you are responsible for right now. Instead of making it all about you and carrying a "woe is me" attitude, what if you approached the wall that is in front of you as an opportunity to let your light shine on the situations you are involved in? This is what makes up the life of a believer: to bring hope where there is no life, to bring light where there is darkness, to restore what has been lost and to rebuild what has been ruined.

Remember in chapter 6, when I wrote about the time my wife and I had three open doors to choose from? There is a little more to the story than I mentioned. Let me give you the background. In 1999, Candace and I got a phone call inviting us to become youth pastors at the church I grew up in. I spent my whole childhood in Weaverville and loved it very much, but I really did not desire to go back. Over the few months following those invitations, though, we eventually decided that this was the next step for us. We moved in August 1999.

My wife was the happiest person around after the move. It had actually been in her heart to live in Weaverville at some point in her life. It was a dream she had had from the time she was a little girl (she grew up two hours away).

The first six months back in Weaverville were bittersweet for me. I loved the mountains and the people, but I was not completely stoked to be back. I felt isolated. After a few months went by, I found myself in a place of not having any motivation. I began dreaming of the day we would leave Weaverville. Before we moved there, we had received prophetic words that we would be there for two years. That only fueled my desire to leave. In many ways, I began counting down the days we had left.

At one point in the first six months, Candace confronted me on my attitude. In this confrontation, I realized that God had put this particular wall in front of me to build, yet I was looking for a wall to build that was not in front of me. As I took inventory of the thoughts in my head, it became obvious that I had allowed the enemy to distract me from what God had for me. Here were some of the thoughts I was entertaining:

- Am I really doing something worthwhile?
- What if I live in this town forever?
- I'm not really a part of the move of God in the earth!
- Weaverville is too small for me.
- No one really is hungry for more of God here.
- No one will recognize my accomplishments, and I will go off the radar . . .

As I look back on these thoughts, I chuckle at the fact that these things went through my head. They were very real to me at the time, however, and it was a tough season to walk through. I was really discouraged. This season became a time in my life when I needed to adjust the attitudes of my heart, and as I worked through that, I began to realize that I had everything upside down. God turned everything right side up. This transition did not take place overnight; it was a process of letting go and completely surrendering to Him and trusting Him. It was revealed to me that I did not trust Him in the measure I needed to. Situations that we cannot control often reveal our level of trust in God.

God was so good to me in that season. He began to expose the lies that I believed and replace them with truth. When you have the truth in you, it does not matter where you are; you will thrive in every situation. Truth is what sets you free (see John 8:32). Carrying the truth in your heart allows you to rise above any circumstance or situation. It enables you to flourish anywhere.

When I turned the corner in this season, I found myself falling in love with the wall that was in front of me. I took complete ownership of it and gave it my all. What happened in the next two years was even more challenging than in the first six months. But I was thriving because of the truth that was in me. I just knew that this was the wall in front of me, and over time, we saw a turnaround in the ministry. Unchurched kids were calling that place their home, as well as giving their lives to Jesus.

We ended up staying in Weaverville for six years total. I do not have the words to fully explain how vital that season was for me. It was a hypergrowth season in my leadership skills, character and ministry. Given my current responsibilities, it is hard to imagine being able to do what I am doing now without having gone through that season. In fact, it scares me even to think about it. I have found through personal experience that the step of learning how to build the wall in front of you is absolutely vital.

God Is a Good Teacher

The fourth step necessary to break free of the fear of man is to realize that God is a good teacher. Think of it this way: We would find it pretty ridiculous if we had an education system where a test was never offered. Imagine for a moment if our DMVs did not require you to take a driver's training test prior to receiving your license. What if they just handed out driver's licenses on your sixteenth birthday? It would be foolish for anyone to think he can pass a calculus test if he has not learned basic addition like two plus two. A good teacher always prepares you for a test. A test is a great way to see where you are in the process of learning something.

One shift that takes place once you realize you are the child of a good Dad is that you approach tests differently. For one thing, you are much better prepared for the tests that come your way in life because God is a good teacher. Let's take a look at a couple passages that give us an idea of the broad spectrum of God's teaching abilities. The first is 1 Corinthians 10:13 (NIV):

> No temptation has overtaken you except what is common to mankind. And God is faithful; he will not let you be tempted beyond what you can bear. But when you are tempted, he will also provide a way out so that you can endure it.

The above passage represents one end of the spectrum. At the other end we have Matthew 25:14–15 (NIV):

> Again, it will be like a man going on a journey, who called his servants and entrusted his wealth to them. To one he gave five bags of gold, to another two bags, and to another one bag, each according to his ability. Then he went on his journey.

Here we have two passages of Scripture that I think paint a broad spectrum about how God is a good teacher. On the one end, you have the temptation part. This passage reveals the truth that there is always a way out of a temptation. Then on the opposite end, we have the parable of the talents. Here it shows that the master gave each man talents "according to his ability." It was never about who had the most; it was only about what they did with what they had been given.

This broad spectrum covers everything from the temptation and sin aspects of life to the gifts and talents God gives us. This helps me see that in every situation, there is always a way to come through it successfully. The issue for many people is that they spend most of their time complaining and grumbling when they face a challenge, and they fail to realize they are in a test that is about to reveal their promotion.

It is unfortunate to enter a test and plan to fail it, though sometimes we simply do not think we will pass for one reason or another. As children of God, we must understand that He is a good teacher and that all the things He is doing in our lives are preparing us to pass the tests we face with flying colors. In this journey of life, with all the many opportunities it presents, it is a good idea to embrace the tests that come up and know that God has equipped us to pass them and thrive.

Self-Promotion Is the Absence of Trust in God

The final step in breaking free of the fear of man is confronting self-promotion. We live in a day when much emphasis is placed on having a mission and vision for your life. I do believe it is important to have a clear idea of what burns in your heart; it is what helps you get up in the morning. My concerns here lie more in the attitude of the person who has a mission and vision, though.

Proverbs 3:5–6 tells us, "Trust in the LORD with all your heart, and lean not on your own understanding; in all your ways acknowledge Him, and He shall direct your paths." I am amazed at how much self-promotion gets in the way of the path God has in mind for us. Self-promotion is the lack of trust in God. Because of various factors, we often feel the need to "do it ourselves." If we were to take a hard look at why we do this, it boils down to our lack of trust in God.

When you and I learn to let God direct our paths, it does not give us permission to lie around and wait for God to do everything. It is about being diligent in everything we do and letting God promote us and open up doors that only He can open. This trust and diligence are what we bring to our partnership and co-laboring with Him.

In a speech to a graduating class at Stanford University, the late founder and CEO of Apple, Steve Jobs, said, "Again, you can't connect the dots looking forward; you can only connect them looking backward."[1] He was sharing that as he lived his life, he was not quite sure where it was going; however, when he looked back, he could see how certain "dots" all connected to help him become one of the greatest innovators in history.

Whenever I am on a plane, I love to look out the window at the earth below. All the creeks and rivers never go in a straight line. They zigzag, which looks erratic from up high. But if you pay close attention, you will notice how easily the water flows and what it does to its surroundings. It brings life. I am sure that if you and I were in charge of determining how a river or creek would flow, we would mark out a course for it that was much more systematic and methodical. That is the beauty of life and embracing every aspect of the journey, though. It is important to realize that sometimes life does not flow in a straight line. To put it another way, it is more about learning to dance as you go than it is about mastering everything before you get on the dance floor.

Back to Coffee

As I encouraged my friend not to let the fear of man hold him back from building the wall in front of him (his job in the business world), our discussion went into defining what constitutes ministry. *Ministry* is such an interesting word in the Christian world. It is usually defined as "the work of God," which in a lot of people's minds equates with working at a church somewhere. I want to challenge that. Now is the

1. "'You've got to find what you love,' Jobs says," *Stanford Report* online, June 14, 2005, http://news.stanford.edu/news/2005/june15/jobs-061505.html.

time for the Church to gain a greater understanding of what ministry is. The Great Commission is not tied to a profession.

To take a quick detour in my narrative, it is not in my heart to devalue or demote church ministry. I have been in full-time church ministry for over seventeen years. I am a sixth-generation pastor. It is in my blood. My issue is not with church ministry, as much as it is with the way we have limited ministry to a church setting. Not all of the Kingdom is in a church, but all of the Church is in the Kingdom. The Kingdom of God is bigger than a church setting; it is about every aspect of life.

It is time for us as the Body of Christ to understand more of what it means for the Kingdom of heaven to touch earth. It is hard to get away from the fact that Christ lives in us and is the hope of glory, wherever we are. Yet so many Christians think the only way to do ministry is in a church setting. If this is what we think the Great Commission looks like, then we have a problem.

Some of us feel as though we have to be teaching, preaching, praying for the sick or feeding the poor in order to "do ministry" (even if it is not inside a church setting). Somewhere along the line, we forget that taking our spouse on a date, paying our bills, loving on our kids, coaching a basketball game, running a business or working in the educational system are also part of advancing the Kingdom. Again, the Great Commission is not limited to a certain career.

Let me propose that just possibly, one of the reasons the Kingdom is not advancing as much as we would like is that we have limited ministry to what we think it is. We have failed to understand the fullness of the heart of God when we define the word *ministry*. It is time to erase the lines and barriers we ourselves have put up and watch the Body of Christ embrace a much broader understanding of what ministry can look like.

What if we approached ministry more along these lines: "It is not what you do as much as who you are"? Imagine if the Body of Christ moved away from being so concerned that ministry is *what we do* and had the mindset that true ministry is the overflow of living out of *who we are.*

One of the challenges, especially for Western Christianity, is that we tend to come up with our own categories for what is spiritual and what is not. Since we all desire to live spiritual lives, we give our very best to those areas that we deem spiritual. Then when it comes to anything we define as not spiritual, that area of our life gets our second best. For example, if you do not view time with your family as being in the spiritual category, then your family will not get the best you have to offer. If you do not view your job as something spiritual, then you might find yourself complaining about it or just working at it for a living instead of doing your job with passion and excellence.

How can we as spiritual beings justify focusing our time and energy on things that are not spiritual? That was the question my friend was asking when it came to his job in the corporate setting. The discussion between us ended around not letting fear determine how much we give to the wall that is in front of us and not limiting the word *ministry* to a church setting.

I have interacted with my friend numerous times since that chat we had over coffee, and in just a few months' time, some incredible things have taken place in his life. First, he mentioned that he felt liberated by not feeling afraid anymore of being put in a box. This freedom from what people would think enabled him to give the remaining 5 percent of himself to building the wall in front of him, which in this case was the business. The fruit of the liberty he now walks in is manifesting incredibly to the point that he has now been put in charge of helping restructure the East Coast division as well. The finances and contracts are multiplying.

Knowing the truth that Christ is in you results in His light shining out of you. One of my goals in writing this book was to unlock something in you that wants out, so that you would not be limited by your paradigm, philosophy or opinions about what constitutes ministry. More important, even, than trying to define *ministry*, you need to spend more time realizing who lives in you. When you realize who lives *in you*, you will be shocked at what can take place because you are not limiting yourself to what you think *you* can do.

My friend may end up working back in a church setting someday, and that desire is still in him. The victory for him today is that he is building the wall that is in front of him and is not allowing a box built by the fear of man to determine how well he does it. The key in this is that he is free to be who he is, and he now recognizes—as we all should as believers—that certain ways of thinking can limit the reality of "Christ in us" shining forth from our lives.

9

—— + ——

Hall of Faith

As I mentioned in the Introduction, as the Body of Christ we are destined to be the most confident people on the earth. Now that we have reached the final chapter, I want to highlight one final time the key points we have covered about all *Christ in you* can mean as you live and work to see His Kingdom come. I also want to look at a couple people who made what is often called the "Hall of Faith" in the book of Hebrews. The way God viewed what they did and credited it to them as faith will give you hope and encouragement. Finally, I will end with a "charge" for you to take to heart as you walk out your call to preach the Gospel, heal the sick and do good on the earth.

Let's first take a look at some of the key points we have talked about:

- In God's image—in chapter 1, we talked about the importance of looking at humanity through the lens that every person on the planet was made in the image of

God. As believers, it is important that we view humanity through this lens, not only the lens of the "Fall of mankind." If we do this, we gain a more accurate picture and perspective of God's view on humanity. That in turn creates in us a genuine love for people and a realization of the death inherent in sin.

- **The greatest mystery revealed**—in chapter 2, we recognized that this truth is a major turning point in human history. The fullness of God resides in His Son, Jesus, who lives *in us* (see Colossians 1:19, 27). This begins to unveil to those around us the reality of God as they see aspects of His Kingdom coming in our lives. *Christ in us* secures our eternity with God and enables each of us to demonstrate His Kingdom in everyday life.

- **The light that is in you**—in chapter 3, we saw that in the gospels, Jesus tells His disciples to let their light shine and let their good works be seen by men. This is a command to do good on the earth. When the Light of the world lives in us, then the world will be drawn to the light. The first thing people who live in darkness look for is light. Sometimes people do not fully realize the extent of the darkness around them until a light begins to shine. Light works best in dark places. How we live our lives and what we do with our gifts and skills can demonstrate this light, wherever we are. The Great Commission is not tied to a specific career or profession.

- **Kingdom now or Kingdom later?**—in chapter 4, we saw that in our journey of seeing the impossible become possible, we can find ourselves in a place of loss or defeat in the same areas where we have seen great victory. It seems to come with the territory, and it is important that in the midst of this mystery, we realize that when we see something in the Kingdom, it means we can have it. One of the keys is that we do not change the subject, but stay seated at the "piano" and do everything we can to learn to play it well.

- **Conviction—the birthplace of confidence**—in chapter 5, we identified one of the key ingredients for walking in confidence: We need to live with a deep conviction of who God is and the importance of His grace, which makes us saints. When we deeply embrace this truth beyond thinking of it as a theory, the natural progression as it takes root in us is that our confidence in who we are in Christ increases.

- **Does God trust you?**—in chapter 6, we learned that our relationship with God is a two-way street; otherwise, it cannot accurately be called a relationship. He is God and will always be God, but He is the initiator of the relationship. We often find that God is silent on some of the major decisions in our lives. One of the conclusions we can draw from this is that He trusts us to make great decisions. A lot of freedom comes when we set our faces toward Him, and in that process, He leads us and empowers us to make decisions with Him in mind.

- **Permission to be great**—in chapter 7, we mapped out the two roads we can travel on in our desire to be great. One road is driven by pride and arrogance, and the other road is driven by confidence. Arrogance is motivated by what it can gain, and confidence is aimed at what it can give. Jesus created an environment where His disciples could grow, make mistakes and even wrestle with who was the greatest among them. He redirected their desire to know who was the greatest by telling them that to become great, they must become like a little child. In the Kingdom, we are given permission to be great and to do great things.

- **The box**—in chapter 8, we faced some confrontation. In this journey of growing in confidence and trusting God, one of the things we must confront is the box we live in that hinders us from doing those things. The box is usually created by the fear of man. Because of the fear of man, we trust man to take care of our future more than we trust God to take care of our future. In this box, we can find ourselves living in "self-promotion" mode, which will cause us to come up short of our divine potential. Now is the time to be diligent in breaking free of the fear of man.

Hall of Faith

We started this book with the life-changing truth of *Christ in you* and how it changes everything about how we live and serve to bring the Kingdom of heaven to the earth. As the book developed, I began to break *Christ in you* down to a personal level so we could assimilate all that it means for us into everyday life. As we play this out practically in our lives, I want to end with a look into God's perspective on faith. In this final chapter, I want to look at Hebrews 11, one of the greatest demonstrations in the Bible of the way God sees our lives. Many call this chapter the "Hall of Faith." In it are some truths that have the power to liberate a lot of believers from a limited or even distorted view of what faith looks like.

As we journey through life, experience its ups and downs and encounter things unforeseen, we always need to remember to do our best to see things the way God sees them. Life is interesting in so many ways; each person seems to carry a different deck of cards. Oftentimes we are consumed with wondering why we were dealt our specific hand. The weight of life's complexities and the reasons behind why things happen or do not should be left for God to carry. You and I can, however, position ourselves in such a way that we come to a place of thriving even in the midst of uncertainty. To do that, we need to avoid making all of life's problems about us. Sometimes it is more about our being in the midst of a problem so we can turn a desert into an oasis. After all, that is how Kingdom-minded believers live.

We must grasp the truth that God delights in the people He created, and He sets things up so that His people can be successful. I am convinced that the Body of Christ is coming more and more into the realization that God trusts us more than we trust ourselves.

The responsibility that you and I carry in this is to make sure we stay in a posture that resembles this type of trust. This enables us to live a life of focus and determination to see His goodness displayed on the earth. As we begin to live out this lifestyle, it will stretch us in the areas of our faith and boldness. I have yet to meet a person walking in faith and boldness who did not first have to confront fear on some level. Faith and boldness will bring us face-to-face with fear. It comes with the territory. When we understand how God sees our lives and how we can move into greater realms of faith and boldness, it will help us face our fears.

Before we look at some of the people mentioned in Hebrews 11, let's look at how that chapter defines faith. The very first verse reads, "Now faith is the substance of things hoped for, the evidence of things not seen." Then verse 6 says, "But without faith it is impossible to please Him, for he who comes to God must believe that He is, and that He is a rewarder of those who diligently seek Him."

Simply put, faith is able to take things that are unseen and make them tangible and real. I have found in my journey of faith that there are times when it is easy to walk in faith, and other times when it seems faith is difficult to find. I have found myself in moments when I can feel faith surging through my body, and then in other moments when I am going through the motions and waiting for faith to kick in. That is why we need to remember that faith is not limited to an emotion or feeling; it is also linked to obedience and action.

There have been times in my life when I have lacked faith and have even felt discouraged, yet have seen a breakthrough take place. I think there are some examples of that in the Hall of Faith, too. The first one involves the mother of Moses, Jochebed. Hebrews 11:23 tells us, "By faith Moses, when he was born, was hidden three months by his parents, because they saw he was a beautiful child; and they were not afraid of the king's command." Now read Exodus 2:1–4:

> And a man of the house of Levi went and took as wife a daughter of Levi. So the woman conceived and bore a son. And when she saw that he was a beautiful child, she hid him three months. But when she could no longer hide him, she took an ark of bulrushes for him, daubed it with asphalt and pitch, put the child in it, and laid it in the reeds by the river's bank. And his sister stood afar off, to know what would be done to him.

I marvel at how God saw what Jochebed did to protect her son. God saw her action as one of faith. I would like to propose that she was simply doing the only thing she could do in this moment. Think about it—Pharaoh had issued a decree to kill all the Hebrew newborn males. Moses' mother hid him for as long as she could, and then the "logical" plan that came to her mind was to send him floating down a river.

I am curious about how many mothers would put their three-month-old son in a basket and send him down the river. If you did that, it would come with a little fear about a handful of things: the child drowning, a predator finding him or the possibility that your child would float completely out of sight and into the Mediterranean Sea. Apparently, this was the only logical way Moses' mother could see to save her son, but it could not have been easy for her.

When God saw Jochebed take action in the only way she knew how, He deemed the moment worthy of a place in the Hall of Faith. This encourages me so much because I know that some of the things I do in life do not feel as though I have much faith; they feel more like "I don't know what else to do, so I'll do this." In this mother's situation, she ran out of options and just did what she could do, and God called it faith.

Let's look at another mother, Sarah, Abraham's wife. Hebrews 11:11 says of her, "By faith Sarah herself also received strength to conceive seed, and she bore a child when she was past the age, because she judged Him faithful who had promised." Now read Genesis 18:12–15:

> Therefore Sarah laughed within herself, saying, "After I have grown old, shall I have pleasure, my lord being old also?"
> And the LORD said to Abraham, "Why did Sarah laugh, saying, 'Shall I surely bear a child, since I am old?' Is anything too hard for the LORD? At the appointed time I will return to you, according to the time of life, and Sarah shall have a son."
> But Sarah denied it, saying, "I did not laugh," for she was afraid.
> And He said, "No, but you did laugh!"

As we read earlier in Genesis, we find Abraham carrying a promise to be a "father of nations." This promise could only be fulfilled through Sarah bearing a son. This journey of bearing a son became a long and at times frustrating journey for Abraham and Sarah. In the Genesis passage, we find Sarah laughing at the very idea of having a son, largely because of her age and her barrenness. She evens denies laughing when God asks. I find this story beautiful because by the time we read Hebrews 11, Sarah is listed as someone who carried faith for the impossible. The story in Genesis revealed that she laughed at the idea, and I love how this shows that even in the face of impossible situations (in which you may laugh at the possibilities), as you go forward, God calls it faith.

In our journey of living out what God has intended and designed for each of us, it is a good idea to realize that we are on God's team and He is on our side. His grace and mercy are so big that even when we feel as though we are failing or falling short, He sees it differently. This should encourage us more than anything in our life or situations can discourage us.

A Final Charge

Ephesians 2:1–10 is a passage that clearly lays out what I want you to walk away with from these pages. It is my concluding charge to you as you finish this book:

> And you He made alive, who were dead in trespasses and sins, in which you once walked according to the course of this world, according to the prince of the power of the air, the spirit who now works in the sons of disobedience, among whom also we all once conducted ourselves in the lusts of our flesh, fulfilling the desires of the flesh and of the mind, and were by nature children of wrath, just as the others.
>
> But God, who is rich in mercy, because of His great love with which He loved us, even when we were dead in trespasses,

made us alive together with Christ (by grace you have been saved), and raised us up together, and made us sit together in the heavenly places in Christ Jesus, that in the ages to come He might show the exceeding riches of His grace in His kindness toward us in Christ Jesus. For by grace you have been saved through faith, and that not of yourselves; it is the gift of God, not of works, lest anyone should boast. For we are His workmanship, created in Christ Jesus for good works, which God prepared beforehand that we should walk in them.

Remember that you are His workmanship and that He designed you to do good on the earth. My prayer is that you will realize what *Christ in you* is and that you will experience it in your everyday life, the way God intended.

Eric Johnson serves on the Senior Leadership for Bethel Church in Redding, California. He and his wife, Candace, are the senior leaders over the local church—Bethel, Redding. He is a sixth-generation minister and has co-authored the book *Momentum: What God Starts Never Ends* (Destiny Image, 2011) with his father, Bill Johnson. He has also co-authored numerous other books. Eric and Candace have a passion to see transformation take place in the lives of people, cities and nations. They have two beautiful daughters who make them extremely proud parents.

You can learn more about Eric and his ministry and keep up with him on the following:

bethelredding.com
Instagram: @ericj76
Twitter: @ericbj

More Must-Have Resources

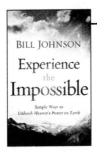

With wisdom and passion, Bill Johnson reveals how to access the power of heaven through the Holy Spirit. His simple, practical insights will transform not only the way you think, act and love but also the very atmosphere around you.

Experience the Impossible by Bill Johnson

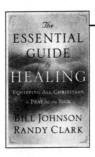

The ministry of healing is *not* reserved for a select few. In this practical, step-by-step guide, Bill Johnson and Randy Clark show how you, too, can become a powerful conduit of God's healing power.

The Essential Guide to Healing by Bill Johnson and Randy Clark

For the first time, Bill Johnson and Randy Clark candidly share their personal journeys behind life in the healing spotlight. With honesty, humor and humility, they recount the failures, breakthroughs and time-tested advice that propelled them into effective ministry.

Healing Unplugged by Bill Johnson and Randy Clark